Table of Contents

INTRODUCTION

ACTIVITIES

APPENDICES

Forest Literacy for All

No matter where you live, you depend on forests. Forests cover 31% of the world's land. They produce oxygen, filter fresh water, stabilize soil, and regulate air temperature. Forests are also home to 80% of land-based plant and animal species and more than 300 million people worldwide.

> **Forest literacy means understanding the value and benefits of forests, and having the tools and knowledge needed to sustain them.**

Project Learning Tree has developed a *Forest Literacy Framework*, which identifies key concepts related to forests. It provides a conceptual outline for both formal and nonformal educators working with K–12 leaners. The concepts are organized around four themes:

1. What is a forest?

2. Why do forests matter?

3. How do we sustain our forests?

4. What is our responsibility to forests?

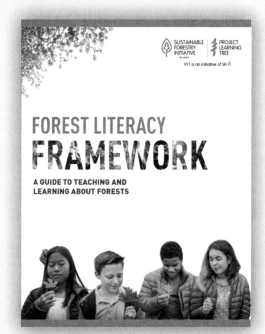

In addition to the concepts, the *Forest Literacy Framework* suggests sample activities and resources for exploring concepts with various audiences.

The *Forest Literacy Framework* promotes education that empowers learners to make critical decisions about forests, to understand the role forests play in addressing environmental challenges, and to grow up to be stewards of forests.

Visit plt.org/forestliteracy to download the PLT *Forest Literacy Framework*.

Introduction

ABOUT PROJECT LEARNING TREE®

Project Learning Tree® (PLT) is an award-winning environmental education initiative designed for educators, parents, and community leaders working with youth from preschool through grade 12. PLT advances environmental literacy, stewardship, and career pathways, using trees and forests as windows on the world.

PLT provides high-quality training, hands-on activities, and multi-disciplinary supplemental curriculum for anyone working with young people. These resources can be easily integrated into existing education programs for all ages and subject areas to help teach youth about trees, forests, and the environment. PLT helps youth:

- develop awareness, knowledge, and appreciation of the environment.
- build skills and the ability to make informed decisions.
- take personal responsibility for sustaining the environment and our quality of life that depends on it.

PLT is an initiative of the Sustainable Forestry Initiative® (SFI), a nonprofit organization that advances sustainability through forest-focused collaborations. Through PLT and other initiatives, SFI supports getting youth outdoors and into nature in ways that inspire them to become environmental stewards and future conservation leaders, and that introduce them to green careers.

NATURE AND YOUNG CHILDREN

Trees & Me is designed to provide opportunities for young children ages 1–6 to experience nature, with a particular focus on trees. Research indicates that early exposure to nature and the outdoors improves emotional and physical well-being, enhances learning, promotes positive social behavior, and makes children more likely to care about their environment throughout their lives.

Trees & Me is an invitation to increase the quantity and quality of nature experiences with the children in your care. It provides fun experiences to explore elements of nature, both indoors and outdoors.

The activities in *Trees & Me* are intended to supplement the learning opportunities you provide for the children in your care. You can use the experiences individually or collectively, adapting them to meet the unique needs of your children, the natural environment in your area, and the materials you have available.

See Appendix A: Engaging Early Learners for helpful guidelines for implementing *Trees & Me* experiences with young children.

(3) **Trees & Me is designed for use with children ages 1–6. Look for this icon for experiences that work well with children under three years old.**

The outdoor icon  indicates outdoor experiences you might try. Each activity also includes a Take It Outside! suggestion for extending the theme into the outdoors. Start by exploring nature right outside your door using simple equipment that is familiar to your children. As children become more comfortable being outdoors, they will naturally want to spend time playing and exploring outdoors. Look for nature in your play area, in nearby parks, and along neighborhood streets. You can also find opportunities to bring nature indoors. See Appendix G: Tips for Outdoor Learning and Appendix H: Bringing Nature Inside for suggestions.

LEARNING ABOUT TREES AND FORESTS

Young children are naturally drawn to trees. Trees are kid-friendly to explore, interesting to learn about, and found around the world.

Trees and forests are also essential assets to people and communities. They shade and cool neighborhoods, and they filter water and air. They give us flowers, fall colors, and lovely scents. And they provide a range of sustainable resources, including wood, food, and medicines.

The experiences in *Trees & Me* use trees and forests as windows on the world to increase children's understanding and appreciation of our complex environment. They aim to build knowledge around the tree-related concepts listed in the Tree Discoveries box below.

TREE DISCOVERIES

Use this guide to build knowledge around these tree-related concepts:

- There are different types of trees.
- Trees and leaves have different shapes, sizes, colors, textures, and scents.
- Trees have different parts that perform different functions.
- People use different parts of trees for everyday products.
- Trees change through the seasons.
- Trees provide habitat for animals and plants.
- Trees and other plants and animals depend on each other.
- A forest is an area of land covered with trees and other plants.
- Many different plants and animals live in a forest.

ONLINE SUPPORT MATERIALS

Visit plt.org/treesandme for additional resources to enhance *Trees & Me* activities, including (1) downloadable Family & Friends pages and Ready-to-Go Resources; (2) videos, webpages, simulations, and more online tools for teaching the activity topic; (3) Reading Is Fun! book recommendations; and (4) standards correlations to Head Start, the National Association for the Education of Young Children (NAEYC), and the North American Association for Environmental Education (NAAEE).

USING THIS GUIDE

PLT activities are designed to be easy to use. They provide background information, detailed instructions for educators, and assessment suggestions for adult leaders.

Each activity in *Trees & Me* centers around a theme. The activities suggest a brief introduction to the activity theme (Introducing the Theme) and a more in-depth exploration of the theme (Featured Experience). Each activity also offers a wide range of experiences for further exploring the theme, organized by these sections:

- **Introducing the Theme**
- **Featured Experience**
- **Group Experiences**
  - » Music and Movement
  - » Reading and Writing
  - » Exploring the Neighborhood
  - » Enjoying Snacks Together

- **Free Exploration**
  - » Art
  - » Outdoor Play
  - » Discovery Table
  - » Math and Manipulatives
  - » Dramatic Play
  - » Woodworking
- **Reading Is Fun!**
- **Family & Friends Pages**

Look for these icons:

⭐ **Featured Experience**

🔗 **Group Experiences**

💡 **Free Exploration**

📖 **Reading Is Fun!**

KEY FEATURES AND ICONS

The following activity features will help you tailor experiences for your particular group and setting.

- Did You Know? Forest Fact—Presents an interesting connection to forests for adults.

- Explore Careers—Provides a way to introduce young children to forest-related green jobs through dramatic play or skill practice. See Appendix D: Career Exploration and STEM Skills.

- Outdoors 🌲—Indicates experiences that are best done outdoors. See Appendix G: Tips for Outdoor Learning.

- ⚠️ **SAFETY!**—Points out safety considerations for a given activity.

- STEM ⚙️—Identifies experiences that enable children to practice STEM (science, technology, engineering, and math) skills. Many also include an engineering challenge, which invites children to use problem-solving skills to design a solution. The specific STEM skill is identified in the activity sidebar. Note that Communication, Creativity, and Investigation are present throughout all activities, so specific instances are not identified. See Appendix D: Career Exploration and STEM Skills.

- Take It Outside!—Suggests a way to extend the theme into the outdoors.

- *Trees & Me* Playlist—Provides musical selections and sound samples to accompany experiences. Activities show scannable QR codes for specific tracks; see plt.org/yc-playlist for the entire playlist. Appendix C: *Trees & Me* Playlist has song lyrics and more information.

- Under 3 ❸—Identifies experiences and books suitable for children ages 1–3. See Appendix A: Engaging Early Learners for guidelines on working with this age group.

ACTIVITY COMPONENTS

OVERVIEW
Describes what the children will do in the activity.

OBJECTIVES
Outlines the teacher-based learning objectives.

ASSESSING THE EXPERIENCES
Guides the educator in assessing the effectiveness of the experiences.

WORD BANK
Provides words to use in conversations with the children.

STEM SKILLS
Identifies the STEM (science, technology, engineering, and math) skills children can practice.

ACTIVITY 10 — Home Tweet Home

OBJECTIVES
Provide opportunities and materials for children to:

- Observe signs of insects and other animals living on, or eating, sleeping, or hiding in trees.
- Observe plants such as mosses and lichens that live on trees.
- Adapt a storyline by adding new characters and sounds.
- Express feelings about trees as habitats through music, movement, and art.
- Incorporate the knowledge they gain into their everyday world.
- Play outside in a natural setting.

ASSESSING THE EXPERIENCES
As you observe the children during the day, note the following:

- New vocabulary. In the children's conversations with you and one another, are they talking about trees as habitat for other organisms like insects, birds, and plants?
- Questions. Are the children asking questions that show an increased awareness of how plants and animals depend on trees?
- New ideas. Are the children drawing new conclusions or asking new questions about trees as habitats that are based on their observations?
- Integration of concepts. Are the children using the idea of insects, birds, and other species depending on trees in their art, play, and other creations, without prompting, in a way that demonstrates understanding?

WORD BANK
algae, forest, habitat, lichen, moss, snag, survival

STEM SKILLS
Communication, Creativity, Investigation, Nature-Based Design (making masks), Problem Solving (squirreling around)

OVERVIEW

Children discover how plants and animals depend on trees.

BACKGROUND FOR ADULTS

From their leafy branches to their tangled roots, trees provide habitats for a diverse variety of plants and animals. A habitat is the place where a plant or animal finds all the things it needs to survive, including food, water, shelter from weather and predators, and space to live and raise offspring. Many physical factors can influence habitat, including soil, moisture, temperature range, and light.

Different organisms need habitats of different sizes. A habitat may be as large as a square mile for a white-tailed deer or as small as a single plant for an insect. A tree may serve as part of an organism's habitat, or it may be the organism's entire habitat. For example, an oak tree may be just part of the habitat for a squirrel or a crow, but to the lichens and mosses growing on the tree, it's their entire habitat and provides everything they need. Trees sometimes serve as a microhabitat, which is a small, localized habitat within a larger ecosystem. A decomposing log in a forest is an example of a microhabitat that sustains a variety of animals and plants.

Even snags (standing dead trees) provide habitats for a number of different species. Tree frogs and beetles live under a snag's bark. Woodpeckers and other birds feed on the insects that live in snags. Chickadees nest in cavities created by woodpeckers. Squirrels and deer mice store food in holes and crevices there.

Take a close look at trees to see the many plants and animals that depend on them!

did you know?

Forest Fact

Forests are home to 80 percent of all land-based plant and animal species!

BACKGROUND FOR ADULTS
Provides relevant information to help you engage learners in the experiences.

INTRODUCING THE THEME

Materials: Tree parts that show signs of use by animals and plants (e.g., leaves with chewed edges, a log with lichens, bark with insect tunnels)

Encourage the children to describe their own homes. If available, use a dollhouse to facilitate the discussion. Ask, "What rooms do you have in your house? What do you do in your house? Where do you eat, and where do you sleep? Do you have a yard to play in? A park nearby that you visit a lot?"

Explain that animals and plants have homes too. We call a plant or animal's home a habitat. Using a real tree or a picture of a tree, ask, "Have you ever seen an animal using a tree as its home or habitat? What animals have you seen eating, sleeping, or hiding in trees?"

Display natural objects that show signs of animals and plants depending on trees, such as fallen leaves, twigs, bark, fruits, or nuts with chewed holes, tunnels, scrapings, cocoons, webs, mosses, lichens, or fungi. Allow time for the children to investigate the objects. Ask, "What clues do you see that show how animals use trees? What clues do you see that show how plants live on trees?"

INTRODUCING THE THEME

Suggests a way to prepare children for exploring the topic.

FEATURED EXPERIENCE: A Nature Excursion

Go outside to find examples of animals and plants that depend on trees or shrubs in your neighborhood. If there aren't many trees, look for ways that plants and animals use buildings, bridges, or telephone poles as homes. Look for the following:

- Animals (e.g., squirrels, birds, insects) living in tree holes or leafy nests, hiding from predators, eating tree fruits or tree parts, and perching or nesting in tree branches
- Vines climbing up tree trunks to seek and soak up sunlight
- Lichens growing on bark
- Mushrooms growing on dead or dying trees
- Snags or fallen trees providing homes for many animals and plants

FEATURED EXPERIENCE

Sparks children's interest through an open-ended exploration or observation.

ACTIVITY COMPONENTS (cont.)

GROUP EXPERIENCES

Suggests group activities that encourage conversation and interaction.

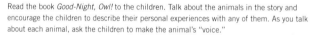

GROUP EXPERIENCES

Music and Movement

** ACT OUT A STORY**

Materials: *Good-Night, Owl!* by Pat Hutchins; animal masks (see Art) or puppets

Read the book *Good-Night, Owl!* to the children. Talk about the animals in the story and encourage the children to describe their personal experiences with any of them. As you talk about each animal, ask the children to make the animal's "voice."

Allow the children to choose which animal in the story they would like to become. Reread the story with the children acting out their parts using animal masks they've made or puppets. Children love repetition. As the story is read over and over, incorporate their improvisations and suggestions for change.

** SING AND DANCE WITH BILLY B**

Play Track 12: This Bark on Me by Billy B on PLT's *Trees & Me* Playlist (scan QR code at right). Invite children to learn the lyrics and dance to the music. See Appendix C: *Trees & Me* Playlist for song lyrics and for tips on using this and other music selections.

Reading and Writing

WRITE A GROUP BOOK

Materials: Animal masks (see Art), crayons, paper, and other book-making supplies

After reading and acting out *Good-Night, Owl!*, ask, "What other animals have you seen in trees?" Encourage the children to choose an animal (e.g., amphibian, bird, insect, mammal, reptile, spider). Invite them to add a page to the story by drawing a picture and by writing or dictating text that follows the pattern of the story. To simplify the story, they can have each animal interrupt the owl's sleep individually rather than cumulatively. Assemble the new pages into a group book, make masks for the new animals, and act out your new story.

TREES & ME: Activities for Exploring Nature with Young Children

FREE EXPLORATION

FREE EXPLORATION

Art

⚙ **MAKE MASKS TO MATCH** *GOOD-NIGHT, OWL!* **STORY**

Materials: Paper plates; hole punch; yarn, string, or elastic for tying on masks; scissors; crayons and markers; construction paper or foam pieces; buttons, craft sticks, feathers, pompoms, or other decorations; glue and tape

Provide dessert-size paper plates with the bottom one-fourth removed. Punch holes in the plate for attaching yarn (see diagram). Supply craft materials and encourage the children to make masks that represent animals. The mask is designed to sit on a child's forehead, with the straight edge of the paper plate resting right above the eyebrows. As a group art activity, you may also wish to design a tree for the story.

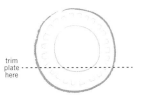

trim plate here

ADD ANIMALS TO YOUR TREE MURAL

In Activity 9: Parts to Play, children made trees by printing with their forearms and hands. Now they can add animals! Encourage the children to draw or cut out pictures of animals from magazines and to add the pictures to their handprint trees. Ask, "What kinds of animals and insects do you think live in trees? Where will your animal live (e.g., on the ground under the tree, in a hole in the trunk, on the leaves)?" Let the children add a variety of animals to the trees.

When they are finished, ask the children to step back and look at their creation. It's no longer a bunch of trees and some animals: this is a forest! Ask, "Have you ever visited a large area with many different kinds of trees and animals? What was it like to be in a forest?"

MAKE A LEAF BACKDROP

Using a large bed sheet, have the children make "leaf prints" by printing on the sheet with their hands dipped in paint. Use washable finger paints so the sheet will be reusable. Vary the color of the "leaves" depending on the season. Let it dry overnight. Use this leaf backdrop for Dramatic Play, picnics, and story times.

FREE EXPLORATION Suggests ways for children to explore topics on their own.

ACTIVITY COMPONENTS (cont.)

EARLY LEARNING STANDARDS

Displays connections to science, English language arts, math, and social studies curriculum standards. Refer to Appendix E: Connecting to Standards.

READING IS FUN!

Recommends children's fiction and nonfiction books that support the activity's theme.

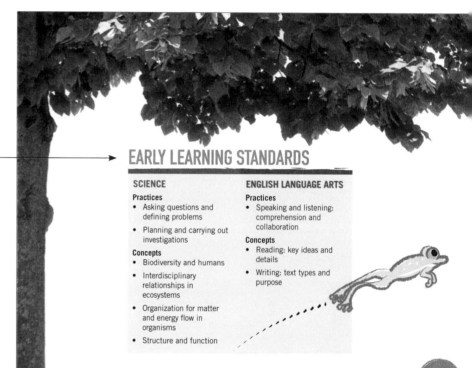

EARLY LEARNING STANDARDS

SCIENCE

Practices
- Asking questions and defining problems
- Planning and carrying out investigations

Concepts
- Biodiversity and humans
- Interdisciplinary relationships in ecosystems
- Organization for matter and energy flow in organisms
- Structure and function

ENGLISH LANGUAGE ARTS

Practices
- Speaking and listening: comprehension and collaboration

Concepts
- Reading: key ideas and details
- Writing: text types and purpose

READING IS FUN!

Bishop, Nic. *Forest Explorer: A Life-Size Field Guide*. New York: Scholastic, 2004. This book is a photo collage that explores and depicts many of the plants and animals that live in a forest. Ages 4–8. ISBN: 0439174805.

Brenner, Barbara. *One Small Place in a Tree*. New York: HarperCollins, 2004. A child watches one tiny scratch in a tree develop into a home for a variety of woodland animals over many years, even after the tree has fallen. Ages 4–8. ISBN: 068817180X.

Cole, Henry. *Nesting*. New York: Katherine Tegen Books, 2020. This stunning picture book follows two robins as they build a nest, keep the eggs warm, and protect their babies. Ages 4–8. ISBN: 0062885928.

Garnett, Jaye. *Who: Peek-a-Flap Board Book*. Rolling Meadows, IL: Cottage Door Press, 2016. Peek and explore in the forest, where you'll meet all sorts of animal friends. Ages 1–5. ISBN: 168052125X.

Hutchins, Pat. *Good-Night, Owl!* New York: Macmillan, 1990. This humorous story looks at an owl's daytime attempt to sleep in a tree shared with a variety of noisy wildlife. Ages 3–8. ISBN: 0689713711.

Sheehy, Shawn. *Welcome to the Neighborwood*. Somerville, MA: Candlewick, 2015. This stunning pop-up book takes readers from neighbor*hood* to neighbor*wood*. It introduces readers to several different woodland animals and explores their unique skills and behaviors that enable them to thrive where they live. Ages 4–8. ISBN: 0763665940.

Home Tweet Home

Things to Do Together

We are exploring the plants and animals that live in and on trees. Trees are great homes (habitats) for birds, insects, lichens, mammals, and mushrooms. Here are some activities you and your child can do together:

- Visit a park or nature center and look for animals living, hiding, and eating in trees.
- Look at trees in your neighborhood for signs of wildlife (e.g., holes, nests, scat, nibble marks).
- Watch a tree for several minutes. How many different animals can you find? Look for amphibians, birds, insects, mammals, reptiles, and spiders.
- Make a flour "trap" to see if animals live near your home. On a smooth, flat board, deck, or off-the-beaten-path walkway, place a dusting of flour. Check for footprints the next morning.

→ Family, Friends, and Forests: Find out what animals live in our state's forests.

Do Your Part

Make a "bug hotel" to provide shelter for beneficial insects. To attract mason bees (which are gentle pollinators), fill a clean, empty soup can with paper straws cut ¼-inch shorter than the height of the can. Hang the can horizontally near a tree or bush. Search online for other ideas.

Help build your child's vocabulary by using some of these new words in your conversations:

_____
_____
_____
_____

We are reading the following books. Check them out from your library, and invite your child to share them with you.

_____
_____
_____
_____

FAMILY AND FRIENDS

Suggests ways that families and friends can enhance their child's learning experiences. Each page includes a "Do Your Part" suggestion for actions they can take together to make a difference in their community.

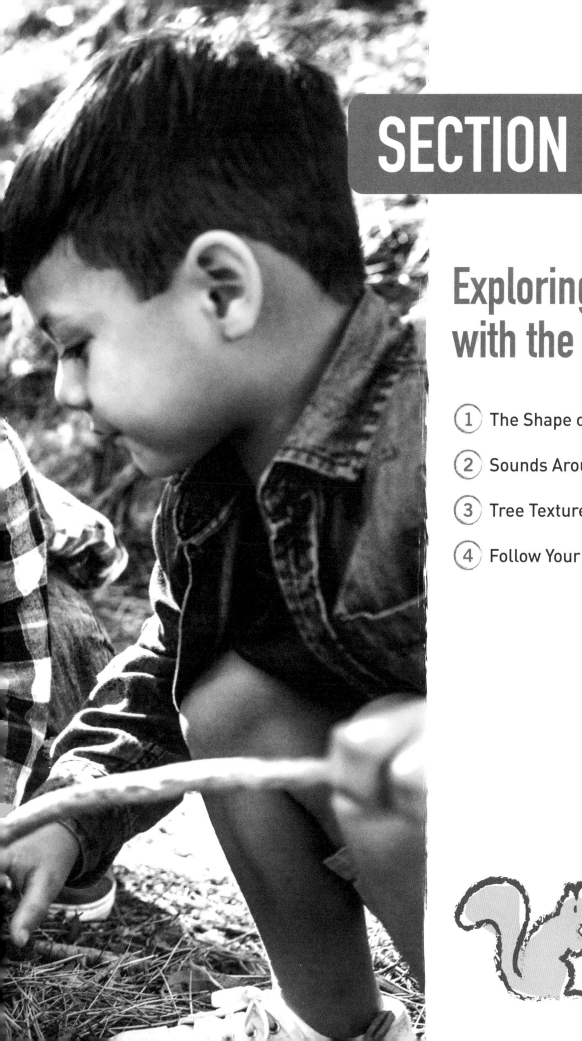

SECTION 1

Exploring Nature with the Senses

The Shape of Things

OBJECTIVES

Provide opportunities and materials for children to:

- Observe shapes in natural and built environments.
- Look at nature in new ways by using tools that they construct themselves.
- Express feelings about shapes in nature through writing, music, movement, and art.
- Incorporate the knowledge they gain into their everyday world.
- Play outside in a natural setting.

ASSESSING THE EXPERIENCES

As you observe the children during the day, note the following:

- New vocabulary. In the children's conversations with you and one another, are they using more adjectives to describe shapes and colors?
- Questions about shapes. Are the children asking questions about the static geometric shapes found inside and in the built environment, and the more fluid shapes found in nature?
- New ideas. Are the children's experiences helping them form new ideas or refine old ideas? Are the older children beginning to recognize that colors have different shades, patterns, and hues?
- Integration of concepts. Are the children using shapes in their art, play, and other creations, without prompting, in a way that demonstrates understanding?

WORD BANK

binoculars, circle, close-up, magnify, observation, oval, rectangle, shape, square, tangram

STEM SKILLS

Collaboration (making shape guide), Communication, Creativity, Investigation, Problem Solving (building shape tower), Technology Use (making and using binoculars)

OVERVIEW

Children search for the shapes and colors that define both our natural and built environments.

BACKGROUND FOR ADULTS

Nature is filled with objects of different colors, sizes, and shapes. These characteristics help us to differentiate, categorize, and identify living things and other items. For example, we can often identify tree species by looking at their leaves' shape. Cherry trees have oval leaves, cottonwoods have triangular leaves, and willow trees have blade-shaped leaves.

The shape of a plant's leaves is the result of many factors. Plants must maximize their ability to absorb the carbon dioxide and sunlight they use to make their food, while also minimizing water loss and damage from wind or extreme temperatures. While roundish leaves are often better at absorbing sunlight than other shapes because of their greater surface area, they are also prone to wind damage. Due to this trade-off, roundish tree leaves tend to be small, like beech leaves, enabling them to strike a balance between maximum light absorption and minimum wind damage. Larger leaves are usually lobed, like oak or maple leaves, as that shape can withstand wind better. Plants in areas where the temperature regularly drops below freezing tend to have needle-shaped leaves, like pines or firs, as that shape has a small surface area and reduced risk of damage from freezing.

did you know?

Forest Fact

The leaf shape of any tree species can vary with elevation and temperature. At cooler temperatures and higher elevation, red maple leaves tend to have more jagged edges, or margins. This helps them to capture more sunlight energy to make food for the tree.

INTRODUCING THE THEME

Materials: Natural objects with defined shapes (e.g., eggs, leaves, nests, rocks, shells, stumps), human-made objects for comparison (e.g., balls, blocks, dishes)

Gather a variety of natural and human-made objects (at least one per child) that have defined shapes. Look at the items together, and sort them into shape piles.

Ask, "What shape does this remind you of?" For human-made objects, ask "Can you find something from nature that matches this shape?"

Many different animal species have shapes or colors, called camouflage, that make it harder for them to be seen. Spots, stripes, and asymmetrical shapes can help break up their body outline. For example, the spots and coloring of a jaguar's fur help it blend into the dappled light of its natural forest habitat. And some animals—such as the orange oakleaf butterfly—are the shape and color of leaves, twigs, or other objects, allowing them to hide in plain sight.

As you facilitate these experiences, be aware of differences in the ways that children perceive the world. If you notice evidence that a child may have color blindness (an inability to distinguish certain colors), nearsightedness (seeing close objects clearly, but seeing faraway ones as blurry), or farsightedness (seeing faraway objects clearly, but seeing close ones as blurry), be sure to alert the child's parent or guardian.

FEATURED EXPERIENCE: Shape Hunt

Materials: Labeled shapes cut from paper (with younger children, use circles, squares, and triangles; with older children, add hearts, ovals, and stars), hole punch, yarn or pipe cleaners

Before the activity, make "shape necklaces" by cutting out shapes from construction paper. (To help children focus on shapes—and to avoid confusion for neurodiverse or English language learners—make all the shapes the same color. See Appendix B: Diverse Learners, Diverse Needs.) Print the name of the shape on each cutout and punch a hole in each.

Hold up each shape in turn and ask the children to identify it. Ask, "Do you see anything in the room that is this shape?"

Give each child one of each shape cutout, and show how to string the shapes on yarn (or pipe cleaners) to make necklaces or bracelets. You could also consider starting with just one shape and adding more shapes over time.

 Take a short excursion outside to look for shapes. When you see an object that looks like one of the children's shapes, hold up the appropriate cutout and say, "I spy something shaped like a ____." Encourage the children to look for that particular shape in nature.

Repeat with the other shapes. Encourage the children to look for shapes on their own and say, "I spy something shaped like a ____." With very young children, add colors to the description (e.g., "I spy something that is yellow and shaped like a _____.")

When you return inside, hold up each cutout shape in turn. Ask, "What did you see outside shaped like a ____? Which shapes did you see the most? Which shapes are your favorites?"

SAFETY! For safety information and other ideas for conducting learning outdoors, see Appendix G: Tips for Outdoor Learning.

Music and Movement

SING WITH LEAF SHAPES

Materials: Leaves from four or five trees common in your area (about two per child), preferably with distinct shapes. Press and laminate the leaves for multiple uses year-round.

Give each child a leaf. Keep one of each type of leaf for yourself. Choose one leaf to hold up. Ask the children to look at the leaves they are holding and compare their leaves with the one in your hand. Ask the children with matching leaves to hold them up. As a group, decide what you will call the leaf shape. Repeat with the other leaves.

Sing the following song and encourage the children to move with the words. The tune is All Around the Mulberry Bush.

> **If you have a star leaf, star leaf, star leaf**
> **If you have a star leaf, stand up now.**

Repeat the verse using different shapes until all the children are standing. Put all the leaves in a pile, and let the children choose a different shape. Review the names for the shapes if necessary. Then sing the song while inserting different ways for the children to move. For example:

> **If you have an oval leaf, oval leaf, oval leaf**
> **If you have an oval leaf, jump up and down.**

DANCE WITH LEAVES

Materials: Leaves from neighborhood trees (laminated for durability) or copies of the Leaf Shapes template in Appendix J: Ready-to-Go Resources, Track 1 on PLT's *Trees & Me* Playlist (scan QR code at right)

Hold up a leaf shape. Ask, "How could you use your body to make this shape? Can you make this shape with your whole body? With your fingers? While you are sitting? While you are standing?" Repeat this process with the other leaf shapes.

Ask the children to scatter the leaves around the play area and to stand among them. Tell the children they will be listening and moving to music. Play Track 1: Shape Walk on PLT's *Trees & Me* Playlist. When the music starts, encourage the children to use the rhythm of the music as their movement guide or invite the children to move around the area like an animal (e.g., scurry like a chipmunk, fly like a robin, or walk like an ant). When the music stops at the end of each segment, hit pause. Each child should find a leaf shape to stand on and create the shape with his or her body. Repeat the process for each music segment on Track 1.

3 SING AND DANCE WITH BILLY B

Play Track 2: Outside by Billy B on PLT's *Trees & Me* Playlist (scan QR code at right). Invite children to learn the lyrics and dance to the music. See Appendix C: *Trees & Me* Playlist for song lyrics and for tips on using this and other music selections.

Reading and Writing

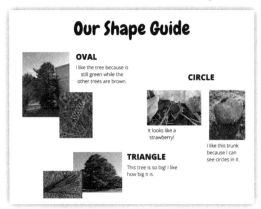

Our Shape Guide

OVAL
I like the tree because is still green while the other trees are brown.

CIRCLE
It looks like a strawberry!

I like this trunk because I can see circles in it.

TRIANGLE
This tree is so big! I like how big it is.

MAKE A SHAPE GUIDE

Materials: Digital camera, digital software for book making

Encourage each child to find a plant, animal, or other natural object outdoors that has an interesting shape. Photograph each object. Back inside, work with individual children to identify the object by shape and type (e.g., oval rock, triangular tree, or round ladybug). Ask the children to dictate why they like the object or share some interesting bit of information about it. Assemble the photos and text into an electronic shape guide, or print a book that the children can take turns sharing with their families.

Exploring the Neighborhood

As you explore the neighborhood:

- Take your binoculars (see Art section) to look for things in nature. The binoculars work amazingly well! They help children focus on one thing at a time and see things they might have missed.

- Find tree shapes. As they grow in a park or open setting, trees of the same species take on similar shapes (e.g., spruces are shaped like triangles, sugar maples and sweetgums are shaped like eggs, white oaks are shaped like gumdrops, and weeping willows are shaped like umbrellas).

- 3 Have children bring a bucket or bag and gather interesting nature objects they find on the ground (like rocks, cones, or seed pods) to use in activities.

⚠ **SAFETY!** For safety information and other ideas for conducting learning outdoors, see Appendix G: Tips for Outdoor Learning.

Enjoying Snacks Together

MAKE AND EAT FRUIT KABOBS

Recipe: Wooden skewers (one per child) or plates or both, fruits cut into shapes (use fruits that are in season, such as apple or orange sections cut into triangles, cherry or banana circles, melon squares, grape or kiwi ovals, or starfruit stars)

Give the children bamboo or wooden skewers and allow them to make fruit kabobs of their favorite fruits, arranging them by shape.

 With younger children, make fruit salad without skewers and invite them to sort and arrange the fruits by shape on their plates before eating.

 SAFETY! Be aware of any food allergies, dietary needs, or choking hazards for the children in your group.

FREE EXPLORATION

Art

MAKE BINOCULARS

Materials: Paper towel tubes, tape, glue, construction paper, paints, stickers for decoration

Cut paper towel tubes in half, and then staple, glue, or tape the halves together to make binoculars. Punch holes in the tubes, and attach yarn to make a neck strap. Encourage the children to decorate the binoculars with paints or stickers. Some children might find it easier to use binoculars with a handle. Glue a wooden craft stick or pencil between the tubes to make the handle.

CREATE SUN PRINTS

Materials: Dark-colored construction paper, tape, objects with distinct shapes

Use dark-colored construction paper to make sun prints. Put the paper next to a sunny window or outdoors in a protected location, and plan to tape down lightweight objects. Encourage the children to find flat natural objects and to arrange them on the paper. Leave the paper in the sun at least one hour before checking, longer for more dramatic results. You can achieve even more dramatic results with special sun print paper, which is available in craft stores.

Take It Outside!

Provide picture frame mats or make them out of cardboard, and encourage children to "frame" something outside. They can hold up the mat in the air to frame trees or other objects in the distance or lay it on the ground with natural objects arranged inside it. Before returning inside, give the children a chance to share the natural "masterpieces" they found or created.

🌲 Outdoor Play

Try these fun outdoor activities related to shapes and colors:

- Hide toy animals in the trees, grass, or both. Provide or make binoculars (see Art section) that the children can use to search for the animals.

- **(3)** Build a "treasure hunt" by hiding natural items like bones, feathers, or pinecones for the children to find. For younger children, play peek-a-boo by hiding items under a blanket or in a sandbox.

- **(3)** Lie on the ground and watch the clouds.

- Provide magnifying lenses for exploration.

Math and Manipulatives

⚙ BUILD A SHAPE TOWER

For an engineering challenge, invite children to build the highest structure they can using small wooden cubes, wooden craft sticks, and paper cups. Ask them which shapes are stronger or more stable. (See Appendix D: Career Exploration and STEM Skills for information about developing career skills.)

MAKE TWIG SHAPES

Provide twigs cut in many different lengths that the children can use to form into shapes. You could also cut twigs so that they are common fractions (e.g., red twigs are exactly half the length of gray twigs).

PLAY WITH TANGRAMS

Print and cut apart several sets of the Tangram Puzzle template in Appendix J: Ready-to-Go Resources, using a different color for each set. Children can reassemble the geometric pieces into squares, rectangles, and many other shapes. They can also use the pieces to create and label their own designs.

Explore Careers

Invite children to explore a green job that uses shapes and colors—**NATURE ARTIST**. Provide toy cameras, paint brushes, easels, an apron, and other art supplies for children to act out being nature artists. You might also make an imaginary artist palette by cutting a piece of cardboard into a palette shape and adding spots of color with marking pens or tempera paint.

NATURE ARTIST

EARLY LEARNING STANDARDS

SCIENCE

Practices
- Asking questions and defining problems
- Using mathematics and computational thinking

Concepts
- Biodiversity and humans
- Interdisciplinary relationships in ecosystems
- Organization for matter and energy flow in organisms
- Patterns
- Structure and function

ENGLISH LANGUAGE ARTS

Practices
- Speaking and listening: comprehension and collaboration

Concepts
- Speaking and listening: presentation of knowledge and ideas
- Writing: text types and purpose

MATH

Practices
- Reason abstractly and quantitatively

Concepts
- Geometry

READING IS FUN!

(3) Carle, Eric. *My Very First Book of Shapes.* New York: World of Eric Carle, 2005. In this split-page board book, children look for the bottom half of a page that matches the top half to make round ladybugs, diamond-shaped kites, and more. Ages 1–3. ISBN: 0399243879.

Dodds, Dayle Ann. *The Shape of Things.* Cambridge, MA: Candlewick Press, 1996. A square is just a square until it becomes a house in this clever book. A circle becomes a spinning Ferris wheel, and a diamond with some string and a tail becomes a kite flying high in the sky. Through rhymes and illustrations, this book reveals that shapes are everywhere. Ages 3–5. ISBN: 1564026981.

Murray, Diana. *City Shapes.* New York: Little, Brown Books, 2016. A young girl walks through her neighborhood, noticing exciting new shapes, from the shimmering skyscrapers to fluttering kites to twinkling stars high in the sky. Ages 3–7. ISBN: 0316370924.

Rotner, Shelley, and Ken Kreisler. *Nature Spy.* New York: Atheneum, 2014. A child takes a close-up look at various aspects of nature, including an acorn, the golden eye of a frog, and an empty hornet's nest. Ages 4–8. ISBN: 1481450425.

Sidman, Joyce. *Swirl by Swirl: Spirals in Nature.* New York: HMH Books for Young Readers, 2011. What makes a tiny snail shell so beautiful? Poetic verse and stunning illustrations celebrate the beauty and usefulness of the spiral shape in nature. Ages 4–7. ISBN: 054731583X.

Thong, Roseanne. *Round Is a Tortilla: A Book of Shapes.* San Francisco: Chronicle Books, 2015. This picture book follows the lives of two young Mexican-American children as they discover shapes all around them: from rectangle ice-cream carts to triangle slices of watermelon. Ages 3–5. ISBN: 1452145687.

(3) *Touch and Feel: Shapes.* London: DK Children, 2013. Toddlers can touch and feel circles, squares, triangles, and other shapes as they explore the fascinating tactile pictures in this board book. Ages 1–3. ISBN: 1465409201.

PROJECT LEARNING TREE®

The Shape of Things

Things to Do Together

We are exploring nature with our eyes! It's amazing how much there is to see when we take the time to look. Here are some activities you and your child can do together:

- Use your child's shape necklace to look for shapes in your neighborhood.

- Play I Spy. You begin by spying a nearby object (e.g., a yellow flower). You say, "I spy with my little eye, something that is yellow." Your child looks around and tries to guess what you saw. Give hints if needed. Take turns spying and guessing. You can play I Spy with letters, sounds, colors, or shapes. Or play this Spanish version of I Spy:

  » "Veo, veo" (I see, I see)

  » "¿Qué ves?" (What do you see?)

  » "Una cosa" (A thing)

  » "¿Qué cosa?" (What thing?)

  » "Maravillosa" (Wonderful [thing])

  » "¿De qué color?" (What color?)

  » "Color, color … " (Color, color …) The person names the color of the object seen, such as "Azul, azul" (Blue, blue).

- Eat circles for lunch. Core apples, and cut them into crosswise circles. Eat cucumber slices, tortillas, bagels, or peas. Tomorrow, eat squares: a peanut butter and jelly sandwich, cheese, crackers, or ravioli.

- After a rain, find a patch of mud. Invite your child to use a twig to draw shapes or to write letters in the mud.

→ Family, Friends, and Forests: Talk about shapes you might find in a forest.

Help build your child's vocabulary by using some of these new words in your conversations:

_____

_____

_____

Do Your Part

Model respect for all living things and outdoor spaces. When you're out exploring, talk with children about putting things back as they found them.

We are reading the following books. Check them out from your library, and invite your child to share them with you.

_____

_____

_____

OBJECTIVES

Provide opportunities and materials for children to:

- Listen to natural sounds made by living and nonliving things.

- Imitate the sounds they hear.

- Communicate using sign language.

- Express feelings about natural sounds through music, movement, and art.

- Incorporate the knowledge they gain into their everyday world.

- Play outside in a natural setting.

ASSESSING THE EXPERIENCES

As you observe the children during the day, note the following:

- New vocabulary. In the children's conversations with you and one another, are they using more adjectives to describe sounds?

- Questions about sounds. Are the children asking questions about the variety of sounds in nature?

- New ideas. Are the children's experiences helping them form new ideas or refine old ideas? For example, are they trying to distinguish bird songs from the sounds made by frogs or other animals? Are they curious about other natural sounds they hear?

- Integration of concepts. Are the children using sounds of nature in their art, play, and other creations, without prompting, in a way that demonstrates understanding?

WORD BANK

chatter, chorus, hoot, loud, recording, sign language, soft, sound, volume

STEM SKILLS

Communication, Creativity, Investigation, Nature-Based Design (creating in recording studio), Problem Solving (making instruments), Technology Use (using paper cup ears)

OVERVIEW

Children explore the sounds of nature and imitate them using their own voices and instruments that they make together.

BACKGROUND FOR ADULTS

Nature provides us with many unforgettable sounds. Breezes rustling through the leaves, birds singing early in the morning, and streams gurgling over rocks are just a few examples.

Listening to sounds of nature is not only pleasant, it is also linked to health and well-being. Scientists have found that hearing nature sounds can physically alter the connections in our brains, reducing our body's natural fight-or-flight instinct and helping us to relax. It can also lower a person's heart rate and blood pressure.

Animals create many different sounds in different ways, including:

- **Vocalizations.** When birds sing, frogs call, and mammals growl, the sound is caused by air moving over the animals' vocal cords.

- **Sounds made with other body parts.** Crickets and other insects make sounds as they move one body part against another (e.g., crickets move a file-like ridge on one forewing against a sharp edge on the other forewing to make a chirping sound). Owls click their beaks. Ruffed grouse rapidly flap their wings, creating a "drumming" sound to attract a mate.

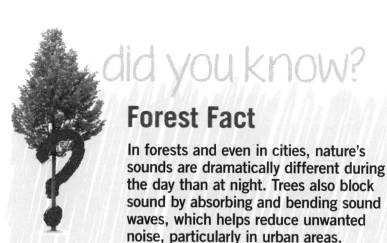

did you know?

Forest Fact

In forests and even in cities, nature's sounds are dramatically different during the day than at night. Trees also block sound by absorbing and bending sound waves, which helps reduce unwanted noise, particularly in urban areas.

PROJECT LEARNING TREE®

INTRODUCING THE THEME

Materials: Recording and playback device, sound-effect recordings, Tracks 3 and 4 on PLT's *Trees & Me* Playlist (scan QR codes at right)

Record the children doing an activity, and play back sections of the recording. Talk about the sounds. Ask, "Whose voices can you hear? What do you think was happening when this recording was made?"

Play Track 3: Neighborhood Sounds on PLT's *Trees & Me* Playlist. Ask, "Where do you think this recording was made?"

Play Track 4: Nature Sounds on PLT's *Trees & Me* Playlist. Ask, "How do these sounds compare with the other recordings we have heard?"

Talk briefly about how sound is produced when something moves. Tell the children to put their hands on their throats and to talk or sing. Ask, "Can you feel something moving inside your throat? How does your throat feel when you sing? Does it feel different when you hum?"

Encourage the children to make different sounds with their voices and bodies. Can anyone in your group buzz, hum, growl, squeak, pop their cheeks, or click their tongues? Ask, "What is the most unusual noise that you can make?"

- **Sounds made with materials in the environment.** Beavers slap their tails against the water, deer stomp their feet on the ground, and woodpeckers peck loudly on wood.
- **Sounds made by movement through the air.** The wings of hummingbirds "hum" and honeybees "buzz" as they fly.

Even different trees make different sounds, particularly in the wind. Some trees "creak" as their branches rub against each other in the wind, while others "rustle" as just their leaves flutter. A swaying oak tree creates deeper sounds than a maple tree because oak leaves are thicker and tougher than maple leaves. The long needles of ponderosa pines make sounds in the wind that writer John Muir described as a "free, wing-like hum," while other pines with shorter, stiffer needles may produce more of a "wail."

As you explore nature with children, enjoy listening to the diversity and richness of nature's music. If you observe that a child has difficulty hearing particular sounds, be sure to alert the child's parent or guardian, as a hearing evaluation may be in order.

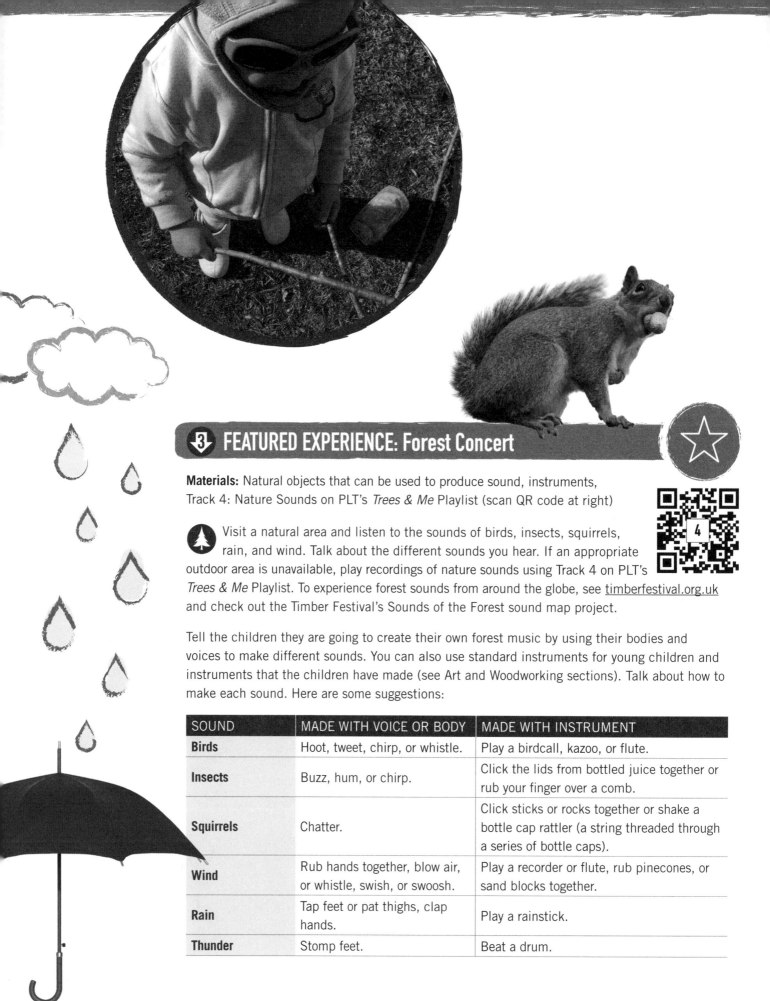

③ FEATURED EXPERIENCE: Forest Concert

Materials: Natural objects that can be used to produce sound, instruments, Track 4: Nature Sounds on PLT's *Trees & Me* Playlist (scan QR code at right)

🌲 Visit a natural area and listen to the sounds of birds, insects, squirrels, rain, and wind. Talk about the different sounds you hear. If an appropriate outdoor area is unavailable, play recordings of nature sounds using Track 4 on PLT's *Trees & Me* Playlist. To experience forest sounds from around the globe, see timberfestival.org.uk and check out the Timber Festival's Sounds of the Forest sound map project.

Tell the children they are going to create their own forest music by using their bodies and voices to make different sounds. You can also use standard instruments for young children and instruments that the children have made (see Art and Woodworking sections). Talk about how to make each sound. Here are some suggestions:

SOUND	MADE WITH VOICE OR BODY	MADE WITH INSTRUMENT
Birds	Hoot, tweet, chirp, or whistle.	Play a birdcall, kazoo, or flute.
Insects	Buzz, hum, or chirp.	Click the lids from bottled juice together or rub your finger over a comb.
Squirrels	Chatter.	Click sticks or rocks together or shake a bottle cap rattler (a string threaded through a series of bottle caps).
Wind	Rub hands together, blow air, or whistle, swish, or swoosh.	Play a recorder or flute, rub pinecones, or sand blocks together.
Rain	Tap feet or pat thighs, clap hands.	Play a rainstick.
Thunder	Stomp feet.	Beat a drum.

GROUP EXPERIENCES

Reading and Writing

 TAKE A LISTENING WALK

Materials: *The Listening Walk* by Paul Showers, copies of American Sign Language Cards template in Appendix J: Ready-to-Go Resources, recording and playback device

Read *The Listening Walk* by Paul Showers (or share a video of *The Listening Walk* with narration by the author, available on YouTube). As you read the story, encourage the children to make the noises in the book.

Before heading outside for your own listening walk, use the cards to teach the children American Sign Language for a few outdoor sounds (animal, tree, bug, wind, rain, and bird). Then, take an outdoor walk and invite children to use the signs to "tell" one another what they hear. Record your walk. Take some time outdoors to listen and talk about the sounds—both natural and human. Ask: "How would you describe this sound? Where do you think it is coming from? What do you think is making it? Can you imitate it?"

When you return, set out the recording and the labeled American Sign Language cards for children to explore. Encourage the children to make new cards for the things they heard on their walk. Visit www.lifeprint.com for an illustrated American Sign Language dictionary.

 SAFETY! For safety information and other ideas for conducting learning outdoors, see Appendix G: Tips for Outdoor Learning.

Take It Outside!

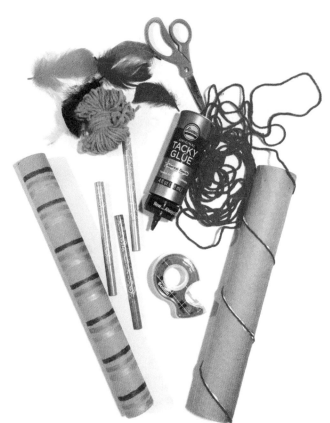

3 Invite children on a "water wander" outside to listen for falling water. After a rain, they will hear lots of things that are wet and dripping. If it has not rained recently, their "water wander" might lead them to a city fountain, a babbling brook, or even an outdoor faucet. Listen carefully for water clues!

FREE EXPLORATION

Art

MAKE AND DECORATE RAINSTICKS

Materials: Empty cardboard tubes about 1–3 inches in diameter (e.g., tubes for shipping, paper towel tubes, wrapping paper tubes); sound bouncers to fill the tubes (e.g., laundry caps, pill bottles, or other clean, hard plastic objects); noisemakers, about ½ cup per child (e.g., beads, dried beans, uncooked corn or rice); cardboard or paper and tape to seal the ends; ribbon, stickers, and craft supplies to decorate

The rainstick was invented in Chile and played to bring rain, but rainsticks make a great sound whether you need rain or not! Cut long tubes in half if necessary. Begin by sealing one end. Then have the children fill their tubes with sound bouncers (see Materials), which should fit inside the tube with room to spare so that the noisemakers can move freely up and down the tube. Add noisemakers. Temporarily seal the other end of the tube. Test the sound. The children can experiment with adding different combinations of sound bouncers and noisemakers. When they are satisfied with the sound, seal the other ends of the tubes and decorate them.

🌲 Outdoor Play

Try these fun outdoor activities related to sound:

-  Cut off the bottoms of paper cups. Show the children how to fit the the narrower end of the cups over their ears. Establish a "no yelling" rule to protect eardrums. Ask: "How do you think your new ears are like animal ears? How are they different? Can you hear any better with your cup ears?"

- Provide birdcalls, and encourage the children to call to each other like birds from different parts of the play area.

- Record the children playing outdoors, and play back the recording inside.

- Make a musical tree by providing aluminum pie tins, large nails, old spoons, metal lids, and other noisy things for children to hang in the tree. Items hung close together will clang against each other. Items spread out with holes or cuts in them will move in the wind and create different noises. Younger children may need help hanging their chosen items.

Discovery Table

MATCH THE SOUNDS

Materials: Plastic eggs or other small containers, items from nature that make noise (e.g., acorns, dried pine needles, grass, pebbles, sand, soil, wood chips), labels

Make two matching sets of plastic eggs filled with items from nature. Invite the children to shake the containers and to find the matching sounds. Number the eggs, and make a chart so the children can record their matches. Ask: "What do you think is inside the eggs? Have you ever heard this sound before? Where?"

Take empty eggs outside and let the children find something to put in them. Experiment with putting the same item in different types of containers. Ask: "How does the sound change when it is inside a different container? What combination of sound and container would you use to make the softest sound? How about the loudest sound?"

⚙ MAKE INSTRUMENTS

Almost anything can become an instrument if played correctly. For an engineering challenge, encourage the children to experiment with combs, pinecones, sticks, metal bottle caps, and other objects. Make a label for each new instrument that says who discovered it, what it is called, what sound it makes, and how to play it. Display objects and labels for the children to experiment.

Dramatic Play

SET UP A RECORDING STUDIO

⚙ Provide instruments, microphones, recording devices, recordings of nature sounds, and blank media. Encourage the children to mix the sounds they make with natural sounds to create new sound recordings. Replay the new recordings and ask the children to choreograph dances inspired by sounds in nature or the music they made.

Woodworking

BUILD INSTRUMENTS

The children can make a variety of instruments:

- Make rattling sticks by cutting a 1- by 2-inch piece of wood about 7 inches long and sanding it smooth. Punch holes in eight metal bottle caps by hammering a large nail through each cap. Loosely nail sets of four caps back-to-back to the wood handle, so the bottle caps can slide on the nail as the stick moves side-to-side.

- Make sand blocks by cutting two 2- by 4-inch blocks of wood and gluing on sandpaper. Rub the blocks together to make sound.

- Make rhythm sticks by cutting and sanding ½- to ¾-inch dowels about 10 inches long. Show the children how to tap the sticks together.

- Make a drum by gluing four pieces of wood together to make an open-ended box. Tape leather, plastic, or vinyl over one end. Decorate the wood.

- Make birdcalls by cutting a piece of wood 2 inches on each side and sanding it smooth. Drill a hole into the wood just a tiny bit bigger than a 16-penny nail. Rub rosin on the nail. When the children twist the nail in the hole, it will chirp like a bird or squirrel.

For more information, see Appendix I: Woodworking for Everyone.

Explore Careers

Invite children to explore a green job that involves investigating the sounds of nature—NATURALIST. Naturalists study and teach people about the natural world. Provide bird identification books (try Fandex Family Field Guides) and sounds (try the Song Sleuth app) for children to learn about nature, then have them practice being naturalists by sharing what they learn.

NATURALIST

EARLY LEARNING STANDARDS

SCIENCE

Practices
- Analyzing and interpreting data
- Developing and using models
- Planning and carrying out investigations

Concepts
- Patterns
- Structure and function
- Wave properties

ENGLISH LANGUAGE ARTS

Practices
- Speaking and listening: comprehension and collaboration

Concepts
- Speaking and listening: presentation of knowledge and ideas

MATH

Practices
- Reason abstractly and quantitatively

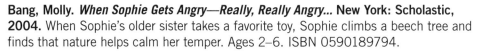

READING IS FUN!

Bang, Molly. *When Sophie Gets Angry—Really, Really Angry...* New York: Scholastic, 2004. When Sophie's older sister takes a favorite toy, Sophie climbs a beech tree and finds that nature helps calm her temper. Ages 2–6. ISBN 0590189794.

Baylor, Byrd. *The Other Way to Listen.* New York: Aladdin, 1997. Presented from the point of view of a young child, the book describes how to listen to the world around us. Ages 4–8. ISBN: 0689810539.

(3) Brown, Margaret Wise. *The Quiet Noisy Book.* New York: HarperFestival, 2017. Originally published in 1950, the classic story of the little dog, Muffin, shows readers of this board book that sometimes the quietest of sounds are the most important of all. Ages 1–4. ISBN: 0062484664.

(3) Carle, Eric. *The Very Quiet Cricket.* New York: Philomel, 1997. A small cricket hatches and is greeted by other insects in this board book, but nothing happens when he rubs his wings together—until he spies another cricket and chirps a beautiful sound. Ages 2–4. ISBN: 0399226842.

Showers, Paul. *The Listening Walk.* New York: HarperCollins, 1999. A young girl takes a quiet walk with her father and identifies the different sounds they hear. Ages 3–6. ISBN: 0064443226.

PROJECT LEARNING TREE®

Sounds Around

Things to Do Together

We are exploring nature with our sense of hearing. Here are some activities you and your child can do together:

- Talk about sounds with your child. List your favorite sounds, nature sounds, happy sounds, scary sounds, and warning sounds.

- Experiment with ways to make music or noise with natural objects. If you find an interesting "instrument," try to find three different ways you can play it.

- Talk about instruments that come from trees (e.g., didgeridoo, dulcimer, guitar, piano, violin). If you play one, invite your child to sing, dance, or clap as you play a song.

- Brainstorm a list of "noisy" foods, and choose a few to eat for snacks or supper.

- Sit or stand quietly outside, and count all the different sounds you hear. Compare the sounds you hear at different places (e.g., backyard, park, playground, street).

→ Family, Friends, and Forests: Talk about sounds you might hear in a forest.

 Do Your Part

Help children learn a few words in American Sign Language or another language new to them. Encourage them to say "Hello," "Goodbye," "Please," and "Thank you" to someone in your community in that language.

Help build your child's vocabulary by using some of these new words in your conversations:

_____

_____

_____

We are reading the following books. Check them out from your library, and invite your child to share them with you.

_____

_____

_____

OBJECTIVES

Provide opportunities and materials for children to:

- Explore natural objects and textures through touch.
- Use words to describe natural textures.
- Express feelings about natural textures through music, movement, and art.
- Incorporate the knowledge they gain into their everyday world.
- Play outside in a natural setting.

ASSESSING THE EXPERIENCES

As you observe the children during the day, note the following:

- New vocabulary. In the children's conversations with you and one another, are they describing the textures they encounter?
- Questions about texture. Are the children asking questions that show an increased awareness of the variety of textures in nature?
- New ideas. Are the children's experiences changing the way they interact with nature? For example, are they initiating contact with nature, more open to handling natural objects, or pointing out new textures to you and one another?
- Integration of concepts. Are the children using texture and trees in their art, play, and other creations, without prompting, in a way that demonstrates understanding?

WORD BANK

bumpy, crunchy, hard, rough, sharp, smooth, soft, spongy, sticky, texture, touch, wet

STEM SKILLS

Collaboration (writing touch book), Communication, Creativity, Investigation, Organization (sorting tree seeds), Problem Solving (making nests and experimenting with sandpaper)

OVERVIEW

Children explore trees and their parts using the sense of touch.

BACKGROUND FOR ADULTS

Imagine touching the smooth bark of a beech tree or the rough bark of a shagbark hickory. Nature exhibits many different textures that can give us information about our environment.

In trees, for example, bark textures can offer clues to unique tree properties. A tree's bark is like skin, functioning to protect it from the elements. The bark of different trees has developed to withstand the environmental conditions where the tree naturally occurs. In general, rough bark offers more protection for trees in areas with harsh seasonal weather changes, as well as in areas prone to forest fires. Smooth bark can act as a defense against insect attacks by reducing the ability of insects to grip a tree's surface, and it is common on tropical trees.

Leaf texture is another characteristic that can tell us about a tree or other plant. Leaves may be rough, smooth, waxy, hairy, or prickly. Desert plants often have waxy leaves, which help prevent water loss. Plants with hairy or prickly leaves may be able to restrict insect movement or cut air flow across the leaf surface, also reducing water loss.

did you know?

Forest Fact

Trees help support many other living organisms, including lichens, which appear most often on tree trunks. After rain, lichens are soft and leafy, but they become crispy when dry.

INTRODUCING THE THEME

Collect a variety of items (see Featured Experience materials list for suggestions) while on a nature outing with the children, or ask the children to bring natural items from home. Display the items and allow the children to handle them.

Ask: "How does _____ feel to you? What part of a tree do you think this is? Is _____ hard or soft? Is _____ rough or smooth? Which texture do you like best? What would the world be like if everything felt the same?"

Young children rely heavily on their sense of touch to gain an understanding of their world. As they explore different textures through touch, young children interpret and learn about objects around them. Experiencing which things are prickly, smooth, or fluffy also helps build their vocabulary. In addition, touch and texture strengthen children's motor skills: gripping, squeezing, poking, and holding increase muscle strength and help children develop stronger hand–eye coordination.

 SAFETY! Be sure to keep safety in mind when exploring by touch outside. Check areas for poison oak or ivy, thorns, or anything that could scratch, prick, or poke children.

FEATURED EXPERIENCE: Mystery Boxes

Materials: Large shoeboxes with lids, box cutter for cutting holes in box, items of varying textures found on or around trees (e.g., bark, cones, evergreen needles, leaves, nuts, seeds). If you are unable to collect these things, use products that come from trees, such as fruits, nuts, paper, and wooden toys.

Make mystery boxes by cutting two circles in the long side of each box so that a child can put both hands inside. (If the lids are attached, you may need to trim and tape the lid flaps.) Set out several mystery boxes and place one tree item inside each box. Encourage the children to reach into the boxes to explore the objects with their hands. If you are working with a group of children, have them sit in a circle and pass each mystery box around one at a time so that each child can reach into the box. You might have children draw a picture of what they think it is before anyone says what is in the box.

Ask, "How does the object feel? What words would you use to describe it? What do you think it is?" Invite the children to remove the lids and to look at the objects. Show the children how to select other objects and put them in the boxes.

If the children are hesitant about reaching into a box, eliminate the box and adapt the activity. Try the following suggestions:

- Allow the children to hold or touch the objects with their eyes closed or open.

- Make a mask by painting the shaded part of a pair of sunglasses with white acrylic paint. Encourage the children to wear the glasses while touching the items so they can focus on touch instead of sight.

- Invite the children to try to identify the objects while using other parts of their bodies (e.g., the backs of their hands, their upper arm, or their cheeks).

GROUP EXPERIENCES

Music and Movement

3 **GO ON A "BIG HIKE"**

Use an updated version of the traditional "Goin' on a Bear Hunt" chant and motions to move children over, through, up, and around many different naturally textured surfaces. Have children repeat each line after you, mimicking your motions. Keep the rhythm by slapping hands on thighs. (For younger children, you might add pictures or objects to enhance their experience.)

> Goin' on a big hike. (repeat)
> I'm not afraid (repeat)
> 'Cause I've got my camera (repeat)
> And a friend by my side. (repeat)
> Oh, Oh. (repeat)
> What do I see? (repeat)
> Oh, look! It's some tall, tickly grass! (repeat)
> Can't go over it. (repeat)
> Can't go under it. (repeat)
> Can't go around it. (repeat)
> Got to go through it. (repeat)

Motion with your arms as if you are clearing a way through grass, and use words or sounds to describe how the texture feels. Repeat this verse as many times as you want. Each time, substitute a different surface that the children must navigate. Some ideas are suggested below. It is helpful to choose familiar places.

> It's a slippery pond.... Got to skate over it.
> It's a scratchy pine tree.... Got to climb up it.
> It's a rocky mountain.... Got to scramble over it.
> It's a mossy forest.... Got to tiptoe through it.
> It's a spiny cactus.... Got to step over it.
> It's some hot sand.... Got to run over it.

Finally, you arrive at a dark cave.

> Oh, oh! It's dark in here. (repeat)
> I don't see anything. (repeat)
> I don't hear anything. (repeat)
> I don't smell anything. (repeat)
> My friend says, "Boo!" (children love to scream this part)

"Run" home by increasing the speed of your thigh slapping, and go back through all the places you've been until you get safely home and lock the door.

> Whew! (repeat)
> I'm not afraid! (repeat)

BE A TEXTURE DETECTIVE

Materials: 12- by 12-inch (or approximate) squares of different textures (e.g., bubble wrap, carpet, corrugated cardboard, sandpaper), Track 5 on PLT's *Trees & Me* Playlist (scan QR code at right)

In a large area, tape one texture square to the floor for each child in your group. Talk to the children about how the different texture squares feel. (For younger children, use only two or three types of squares.) Play Track 5: Getting in Touch with Trees on PLT's *Trees & Me* Playlist, while the children move barefoot from square to square. Tell them to stop on a square when the music stops. Teach children a simple call and response. For example, you can ask, "Who is standing on a bumpy square?" and those who can answer, "I am standing on a bumpy square!"

Reading and Writing

 ### WRITE A TOUCH BOOK

Ask the children to talk about animals, plants, and other things in nature that they have touched. Begin by focusing on the items in the mystery boxes and things the children have seen when exploring the neighborhood. Ask, "How did it feel to touch a _____?" Help the children use texture words to describe things in nature.

Encourage each child to write and illustrate a page for a group book. Follow a question-and-answer format such as: "Did you ever have a chick nestle in your lap? How did it feel? Puffy. Peeping. Fluffy. Sleeping." On each page, include text such as "Did you ever touch a _____? How did it feel? _____" and have the children provide the missing text.

Enjoying Snacks Together

EAT TEXTURED TRAIL MIX

Recipe: Tree nuts (e.g., almonds, cashews, walnuts), candy-coated chocolate pieces (chocolate comes from trees!), dried tree fruits (e.g., apples, apricots, cherries), oat cereal, raisins, pretzels

Mix together two or three fruits, nuts, or dry snack foods in a large bowl. Let each child scoop out an appropriate measure of the mixture to eat. While they are eating, ask the children how the different foods feel on their tongues (e.g., crunchy, smooth, mushy, rough). This is a good snack to eat outdoors or on a hike.

 SAFETY! Be aware of any food allergies, dietary needs, or choking hazards for the children in your group.

FREE EXPLORATION

Art

 PAINT WITH TREE-TEXTURED PAINT

Add sawdust, crumbled leaves, coffee grounds, nutmeg, or cinnamon to tempera paint. Use the textured paints to make pictures of trees, hills, or other scenes in nature. This type of tactile exploration may also be used to further engage learners with limited vision or cognitive disabilities. See Appendix B: Diverse Learners, Diverse Needs.

Take It Outside!

Tape large sheets of paper to tree trunks with masking tape. Have the children rub the side of a crayon back and forth across the paper. The pattern of the bark should begin to show on the paper. Label the rubbings with the real or made-up names of the trees. Talk about the patterns that appear. Ask, "How are the patterns different? How are the patterns the same?" Use the rubbings in collages or frame them as artwork.

🌲 Outdoor Play

Try these fun outdoor activities related to texture:

- **3** Walk barefoot in a safe place.

- Provide a variety of textured squares. Encourage the children to look for something outdoors that feels similar to each type of texture.

- **3** Fill a sandbox or raised bed box with sawdust, wood chips, or wood shavings. Encourage the children to hide natural objects in the box and then search for them with small garden tools or their hands.

- Encourage tree hugs!

- Make rubbings of bricks, buildings, sidewalks, and trees.

- Lie in the grass and feel the earth under your back. Close your eyes and describe how the air or wind feels on your face.

Discovery Table

⚙ MAKE A NEST

Provide a variety of nest-building materials like cotton balls, shredded paper, grass, moss, or twigs, as well as small boxes or plastic tubs. As an engineering challenge, invite children to make the softest nest they can for a baby bird, using a tub or box as the base. Encourage them to describe the texture of their nest, and to image what it would be like to sit in it.

Math and Manipulatives

 SORT TREE SEEDS

Purchase or collect a variety of large seeds (e.g., acorns, almonds, buckeyes, basswood seeds, hickory nuts, maple seeds, pecans, sweet gum pods, or walnuts). Place the seeds in mystery boxes (see Featured Experience). Challenge the children to put a collection of seeds into the box and to sort them by touch only. They can remove the box lid to examine the sorted piles. This activity can be done with assorted evergreen cones instead.

⚠ **SAFETY!** Be aware of any food allergies or choking hazards for the children in your group.

Woodworking

 EXPERIMENT WITH SANDPAPER

Provide different grades of sandpaper and different kinds of scrap lumber or tree branch cross-sections. Encourage children to use the sandpaper on different pieces of wood to find which sandpaper is best for smoothing which wood. Provide work gloves if splinters are a concern. Ask, "Which kind of sandpaper do you think will make the wood the smoothest? What happened when you rubbed the sandpaper on the wood? How smooth can you make the different kinds of wood? Can you feel a difference?" For more information, see Appendix I: Woodworking for Everyone.

Explore Careers

Invite children to explore a green job that involves tree textures—ARBORIST. Arborists (or "tree doctors") are trained to care for individual trees. They inspect trees for signs of disease and may even climb into the branches as needed. Find a tree with branches low to the ground and help children safely climb to the lowest one. (Be sure to spot them.) Encourage them to look at the tree's many parts along the way, just like a real arborist would!

⚠ **SAFETY!** This activity should only be done under close adult supervision. Make sure the tree has no rotten roots, cracks or splits in the trunk, or fungus growing on the trunk. Avoid conifer trees like pines, as they tend to have sticky sap and brittle branches.

ARBORIST

EARLY LEARNING STANDARDS

SCIENCE

Practices
- Planning and carrying out investigations

Concepts
- Patterns
- Resources
- Structure and function
- Systems and system models

ENGLISH LANGUAGE ARTS

Practices
- Speaking and listening: comprehension and collaboration

Concepts
- Speaking and listening: presentation of knowledge and ideas
- Writing: text types and purpose

MATH

Practices
- Reason abstractly and quantitatively

READING IS FUN!

③ Colombe, Rose. *Forest: Touch and Feel.* Rolling Meadows, IL: Cottage Door Press, 2019. Smell the raccoon's spruce tree, touch the owl's feathers, and feel the bear's sticky honey. Meet different forest friends in this sense-filled interactive book. Ages 1–3. ISBN: 1680527371.

Cottin, Menena, and Rosana Faria. *The Black Book of Colors.* Toronto, ON: Groundwood Books, 2008. Colors are described by blind children, as they use other senses to tell how the colors smell, sound, taste, or feel. This book features raised images printed with black ink on black paper and the text is printed with both Braille and English words. Ages 4–8. ISBN: 0888998732.

Ehlert, Lois. *Nuts to You!* Orlando, FL: Voyager Books, 2004. Learn about the misadventures of a rascally city squirrel who sneaks inside an apartment window. Textural illustrations depict the story, while labels on each page identify plants, birds, and insects. Ages 3–7. ISBN: 0152050647.

Luyken, Corinna. *The Tree in Me.* New York: Dial, 2021. Through poetic text and exquisite illustrations of children reveling in nature, this picture book explores the various ways that human beings are strong and connected to others—just like trees. Ages 4–8. ISBN: 593112598.

Snyder, Betsy E. *Have You Ever Tickled a Tiger?* New York: Random House, 2009. This book asks if readers have ever kissed a walrus, poked a penguin, or hugged an octopus, among others. Rhyming couplets accompany illustrations with textures to feel. Ages 1–4. ISBN: 0375843965.

Wenzel, Brendan. *A Stone Sat Still.* San Francisco: Chronicle Books, 2019. This is the story of a seemingly ordinary rock—but to the animals around it, it is a resting place, a kitchen, a safe haven, and even an entire world. The narrative and textural illustrations explore perspective, perception, and the passage of time. Ages 3–5. ISBN: 1452173184.

PROJECT LEARNING TREE®

Tree Textures

Things to Do Together

We are exploring our sense of touch by feeling all kinds of natural things. Here are some activities you and your child can do together:

- Make a secret sock by putting a cup in a large sock. Hide something inside the cup, and let your child reach in and feel the object. Encourage him or her to describe it and to guess what it is before peeking.

- Practice using texture words to describe things in and around your home, such as smooth, hard, soft, bumpy, scratchy, or squishy.

- Touch different tree barks to compare their textures.

- Take a texture outing around your neighborhood to collect interesting objects that have fallen from trees. Talk about how the objects feel, and describe them with adjectives such as rough, bumpy, prickly, or slippery. Choose the texture that is your favorite.

→ Family, Friends, and Forests: Talk about different textures you might find in a forest—hard, soft, scratchy, and so on.

 Do Your Part

> **Not everything in nature is safe to touch. Learn together about things children should avoid touching (poison oak, poison ivy, thorns, etc.) and encourage children to teach others.**

Help build your child's vocabulary by using some of these new words in your conversations:

_____

_____

_____

_____

We are reading the following books. Check them out from your library, and invite your child to share them with you.

_____

_____

_____

_____

Follow Your Nose

OBJECTIVES

Provide opportunities and materials for children to:

- Taste tree fruits.
- Smell different tree parts.
- Cook and eat applesauce.
- Write about an imaginary apple tree.
- Express feelings about the taste and smell of natural objects through music, movement, and art.
- Incorporate the knowledge they gain into their everyday world.
- Play outside in a natural setting.

ASSESSING THE EXPERIENCES

As you observe the children during the day, note the following:

- New vocabulary. In the children's conversations with you and one another, are they using new adjectives or combining words in new ways to describe smells or tastes?
- Questions about smell and taste. Are the children asking questions that show they are thinking about the sources of smells and tastes? Are they asking permission before tasting new things?
- New ideas. Are the children's experiences helping them form new ideas or refine old ideas? Are they willing, interested, or excited about smelling and tasting unfamiliar tree parts? Do they seek out new outdoor smells?
- Integration of concepts. Are the children using concepts related to smell and taste in their art, play, and other creations, without prompting, in a way that demonstrates understanding?

WORD BANK

bitter, core, odor, peel, potpourri, resin, scent, seed, skin, smell, sour, sweet, taste

STEM SKILLS

Communication, Creativity, Data Analysis (charting reactions), Investigation, Technology Use (cooking applesauce)

OVERVIEW

Children explore trees and tree parts using their senses of smell and taste.

BACKGROUND FOR ADULTS

Nature provides us with many smells and tastes to enjoy. Different tree species may feature aromatic woods, savory spices, scented flowers, or yummy fruits.

If you've ever smelled pine trees or the sweet, spicy scent of a sassafras tree, you may have wondered what makes them smell the way they do. The answer lies in a group of chemicals that work to lure pollinators and deter predators. Strong-smelling leaves, bark, and flowers are often rich in these natural chemicals, many of which emit powerful scents.

Forests provide a variety of food products with a range of delightful smells and tastes. These include fruits (edible berries, pawpaw), nuts (hickory, black walnut, chestnut), and mushrooms. Real maple syrup also comes from forests and is made from the sap of sugar maple trees, boiled down to concentrate the flavor.

did you know?

Forest Fact

A good sense of smell is very important to many forest animals. Many leave odors on trees and rocks to mark their territory. Others, like skunks, can spray bad-smelling odors up to 15 feet away to ward off predators.

INTRODUCING THE THEME

Materials: Pleasant-smelling items (e.g., candle, incense, pine resin, potpourri), chart paper, marker (scented, if possible!)

Before the children arrive, fill the room with a pleasant smell:

• Heat potpourri.

• Put a few drops of pine resin in water and bring it to a boil. Boiling or heating releases the pine scent.

• Burn a naturally scented candle or incense.

As a group, make a list of smells that the children like and another list of smells that they don't like. Try to focus on natural smells. On a different day, you might repeat with tastes, focusing on foods from trees.

 SAFETY! Be aware of any allergies or sensitivities for the children in your group, and use caution when handling hot liquids and candles.

In humans, the senses of smell and taste are so closely linked that it is sometimes hard to tell them apart. In fact, our sense of taste is mostly about smell. Taste buds on our tongues can only distinguish five basic flavors: bitter, salty, savory, sour, and sweet. All other nuances of taste come from our sense of smell.

Have you ever noticed how a simple odor, such as baking cookies, can bring back a flood of memories? That's because the parts of the brain that process memory, emotion, and smell are located near each other, connecting certain scents with certain emotional memories.

Have fun exploring the smells and tastes of trees!

 SAFETY! Ensure that children only taste items like fruits, tree nuts, spices, or maple syrup from a safe source (such as a grocery store, farm, garden, or farmers' market). Teach children never to eat or taste things without checking with an adult first. Some berries, flowers, seeds, leaves, and mushrooms are highly poisonous, allergenic, or otherwise harmful, especially for small bodies.

FEATURED EXPERIENCE: Applesauce

⚙ PREPARE APPLESAUCE

Materials: 1 apple for each child, cutting surfaces (plates, paper towels, or cutting boards), tools for investigating raw apples (plastic knives or pumpkin-carving knives, magnifying lenses, tweezers), tools for prepping apples (knife, peeler, corer, slicer, or hand-crank apple peeler), slow cooker, sugar and spices (optional), bowls, tools for smashing and eating cooked apples (such as fork, spoon, table knife, and chopstick, for each child)

Divide children into small groups and give each child an apple to examine. Provide magnifying lenses and plastic knives or pumpkin-carving knives so they can investigate the apples. Invite them to use tweezers to remove the seeds and to count them. Ask, "Do all apples have the same number of seeds?"

As the children finish their investigations, adults can finish peeling the apples by hand or can put the apples on a hand-crank apple peeler so the children can peel them. Use an apple slicer or corer and knife to section and core the apples. Talk about what you are doing as you do it, using words like peel, skin, core, half, quarter, and seeds. Use one of the following recipes to prepare applesauce.

Slow cooker applesauce

Recipe: 1 apple per child, 1 teaspoon brown sugar per apple (optional), 3 tablespoons water per apple, cinnamon, cloves, nutmeg, or allspice

Show the children how to use their knives to cut the apple sections into small pieces. When all the apples are ready, invite the children to help you put the apple pieces in a slow cooker. Measure and add water. You can also add sugar and spices, if desired. Allow the mixture to simmer until the apples are soft (approximately 3-4 hours). Check on the apples during the day to watch the cooking process. Spoon the cooked apples into bowls.

Provide each child with a variety of tools, such as a fork, a spoon, a table knife, and a chopstick. As an engineering challenge, encourage children to determine which tool works best for smashing the apples and which is best for eating the applesauce.

No-cook blender applesauce

Recipe: 6–7 small apples, ½ cup sugar or honey (optional), dash of cinnamon, 2–4 tablespoons of water

Peel and cut apples. Mix all ingredients in a blender until smooth.

 SAFETY! Be aware of any food allergies, dietary needs, or choking hazards for the children in your group.

GROUP EXPERIENCES

Music and Movement

MAKE "APPLESAUCE"

Materials: Long rope or masking tape to make a large circle on the floor

Arrange the rope in a circle on the floor to form a large "pot." The children are the "apples." You are the "cook." Add the apples to the pot one at a time. You can physically pick them up and put them in the pot or you can say, "If you are wearing red (yellow, green) today, jump into the pot." When you turn up the heat, the apples start to bubble and boil. Pretend to turn the heat up and down so the children alternate between wild boiling, mild simmering, and silent waiting. Stir the apples during the cooking process. Finally, add spices and "taste" the final product.

 #### SMELL THE FLOWERS

Materials: Paper flowers, essential oils, Track 6 on PLT's *Trees & Me* Playlist (scan QR code at right)

Apply a scent to paper flowers with a tree-based essential oil, such as cinnamon, eucalyptus, or pine. Tape the flowers to the floor. Play Track 6: Flight of the Bumblebee on PLT's *Trees & Me* Playlist. Encourage the children to "fly" around the room and buzz like bees while the music is playing. Stop the music several times and have the children find a flower, bend down, and smell it.

Reading and Writing

IMAGINE YOUR OWN FRUIT TREE

Read *Pie in the Sky* by Lois Ehlert or *How to Make an Apple Pie and See the World* by Marjorie Priceman. Invite children to paint or draw pictures of what they would do if they had their very own apple, cherry, or other fruit tree. Talk with each child and encourage him or her to label the picture and dictate the story.

PROJECT LEARNING TREE®

Art

DRAW WITH CINNAMON STICKS

Older children can draw using cinnamon sticks on emery paper or fine sandpaper. Look for emery paper and bags of cinnamon sticks in craft stores.

PAINT WITH SCENTED PAINTS

Mix extracts or aromatic oils into tempera paints. Match scents to colors (e.g., peppermint in red paint and vanilla in white paint), use seasonal scents (mint in spring and cinnamon in fall), or simply feature a smell of the week.

3 MAKE POTPOURRI

Experiment with mixing dried fragrant things. Children can dry leaves, fruit peels, and individual flower petals by spreading them on old window screens and then placing them in a dry, dark place. For younger children, place dried ingredients in separate containers and let them use a scoop to take some of each, creating their own mixture in a bag or bowl. Try any combination of the following:

- Cedar or other wood chips
- Spices (e.g., allspice, anise, cinnamon sticks, cloves, nutmeg)
- Conifer needles and small cones
- Dried tree fruit peels (e.g., grapefruit, lemon, lime, orange)
- Dried flower petals (e.g., apple blossoms, carnations, lilacs, marigolds, orange blossoms, roses, violets). Ask your local florist for discarded flowers.
- Dried aromatic plants (e.g., lavender, lemongrass, mint, orange leaves, rose geranium leaves)

Take It Outside!

Create a scent trail outside. Take half an onion and rub the cut side on surfaces such as tree trunks, rocks, flower beds, and fence posts to leave a trail of onion scent. (Avoid furniture, building walls, or other valuable surfaces.) You may want to leave a note, toy, or treasure at the end of the trail so children will know when they reach it. Invite children to sniff with their noses to try to follow the trail.

🌲 Outdoor Play

Try these fun outdoor activities related to scent:

- **3** Play with scented bubbles.

- Make perfume with flower petals. On a sunny day, show the children how to break flower petals into small pieces. (You can often get discarded flowers from churches, florists, or supermarkets.) Pour a little water on the petals and let them "cook" in the sun for a few hours. Put a small number of flower petals in a zip-top sandwich bag. Close the bag and invite the children to crush the petals with their fingers. Pour the fragrant liquid in a bottle or spray pump. Children can spray the perfume on paper or coffee filters and then wave it around to spread the scent in the air. Experiment with different combinations of flowers for different perfumes. Back inside, use mailing labels to design labels for the bottles.

- Plant an herb garden inside in pots or outside in the ground. Herbs can be grown all winter in a sunny window.

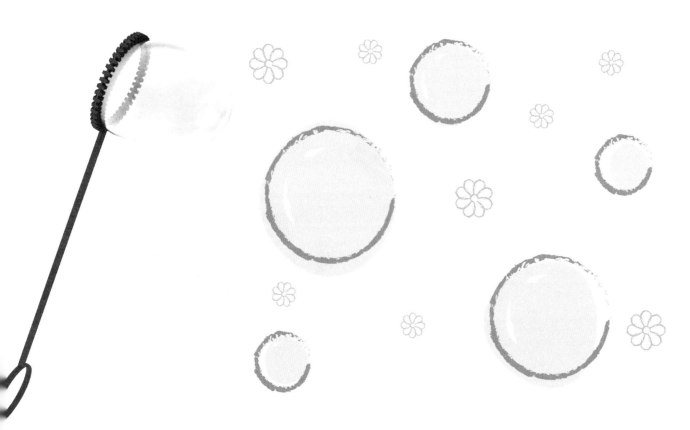

Discovery Table

 CHART REACTIONS TO SMELLS

Put small amounts of fragrant tree products (e.g., apple cider vinegar, cinnamon, cloves, cocoa, coffee, lemon, orange) into small bottles or other containers with lids. Add a cotton ball to containers that have liquids. Put small squares of clean nylon over the tops of the containers. Drill one hole in each lid, and then secure the lids over the nylon. Number each container. You may want to adjust the number of smells as needed for your group. Make a chart on which children can record their reactions to each numbered smell by drawing smiley faces, sad faces, or confused faces. Show them how to smell unfamiliar or strong smells by waving their hand over the smell instead of inhaling them directly. Ask, "Which smells do you recognize? Where were you when you smelled them? What do you think about when you smell this one?"

Woodworking

 SMELL SOME WOOD

Some types of wood smell really good! Find or purchase some pine or aromatic cedar boards. Encourage the children to sand the boards. Older children may also shave or saw them. Ask, "Which kind of wood do you think smells best? Does the wood smell stronger when you sand it or when you saw it?" For more information, see Appendix I: Woodworking for Everyone.

Explore Careers

Invite children to explore a green job that involves smelling and tasting—CHEF. Provide tree fruits and nuts with unique smells and tastes, as well as kitchen items made from trees (spoons, bowls, and cookware), and invite children to role play the preparation of a delicious tree-based meal. Compliments to the chef!

CHEF

EARLY LEARNING STANDARDS

SCIENCE

Practices
- Asking questions and defining problems
- Developing and using models
- Planning and carrying out investigations

Concepts
- Natural resources

ENGLISH LANGUAGE ARTS

Practices
- Speaking and listening: comprehension and collaboration

Concepts
- Speaking and listening: presentation of knowledge and ideas
- Reading: key ideas and details
- Writing: text types and purpose

MATH

Practices
- Reason abstractly and quantitatively

Concepts
- Measurement and data

READING IS FUN!

③ Carle, Eric. *The Very Hungry Caterpillar's Garden Picnic, A Scratch-and-Sniff Book.* New York: World of Eric Carle, 2020. This board book tells a sweet story about Eric Carle's classic character eating through his favorite foods, and includes six scents for added fun. Ages 1–3. ISBN: 0593097041.

Corr, Christopher. *Deep in the Woods.* London: Francis Lincoln Children's Books, 2017. A little wooden house, with nine neat windows and a red front door, lies deep in the woods. When a little mouse decides it will make the perfect home, so do the other animals—including a big bear! See what happens next in this retelling of a classic Russian folk tale. Ages 3–6. ISBN: 1847807267.

Ehlert, Lois. *Pie in the Sky.* Orlando, FL: Harcourt Children's Books, 2004. A father and child watch the cherry tree in their backyard, waiting until they have ripe cherries to bake in a pie. The book includes a recipe for cherry pie. Ages 3–7. ISBN: 0152165843.

Mortensen, Lori. *In the Trees, Honey Bees!* Nevada City, CA: Dawn, 2009. This introduction to a wild colony of honeybees offers close-up views of the queen, the cells, and even bee eggs, and an understanding of their lives. Ages 4–10. ISBN: 1584691158.

Priceman, Marjorie. *How to Make an Apple Pie and See the World.* New York: Dragonfly Books, 1996. From the jungles of Sri Lanka to the apple orchards of Vermont, the energetic little baker searches far and wide to find the finest ingredients for her apple pie. Use a globe or map to add a social studies element to the story. Ages 4–8. ISBN: 0679880836.

PROJECT LEARNING TREE®

Follow Your Nose

Things to Do Together

We are exploring nature with our senses of smell and taste. Here are some activities you and your child can do together:

- Cook something together. Talk about where the ingredients come from.
- Open kitchen cupboards and smell things inside.
- Taste without seeing or smelling. While your child's eyes are closed, hold your child's nose closed and offer something to taste. Does food taste the same when you can't see it, or when you can't smell it?
- Talk about smells that can warn us of danger, such as smoke, natural gas, and rotten food.
- Try a new tree food together (such as cashew, kiwi, olive, pine nut, pomegranate, star fruit, or walnut).

→ **Family, Friends, and Forests:** Find out what foods come from forests.

Do Your Part

Make a favorite family recipe that uses a fruit, nut, or spice from a tree. Encourage children to share it with someone else in the community and tell them what makes it special.

Help build your child's vocabulary by using some of these new words in your conversations:

_____
_____
_____

We are reading the following books. Check them out from your library, and invite your child to share them with you.

_____
_____
_____
_____

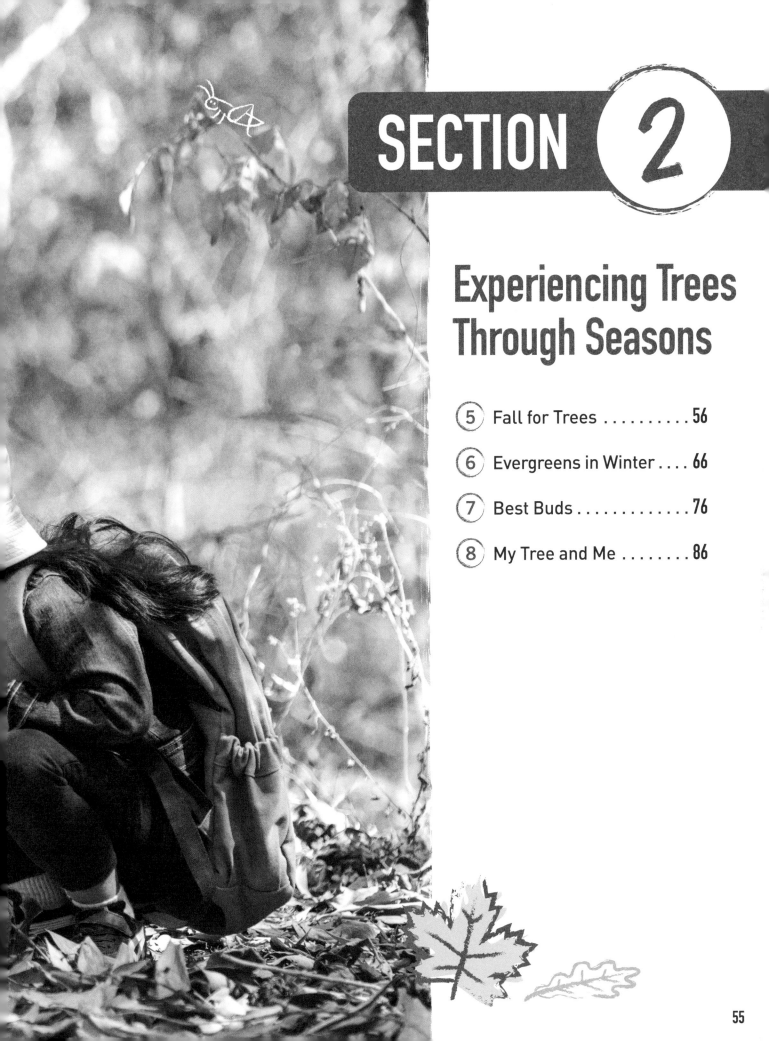

SECTION 2

Experiencing Trees Through Seasons

OBJECTIVES

Provide opportunities and materials for children to:

- Observe seasonal changes in nature, especially fall leaves.

- Collect, sort, classify, and count fall leaves and seeds.

- Write and illustrate a group story.

- Express feelings about fall through music, movement, and art.

- Incorporate the knowledge they gain into their everyday world.

- Play outside in a natural setting.

ASSESSING THE EXPERIENCES

As you observe the children during the day, note the following:

- New vocabulary. In the children's conversations with you and one another, are they using new words to talk about fall and leaves?

- Questions about fall. Are the children asking questions that show an increased awareness of changing daylight, falling temperatures, changes in plants and animals, and changes in their own activities?

- New ideas. Are the children's experiences helping them form new ideas or refine previous ideas? Are they drawing new conclusions or asking new questions that are based on their observations of fall and leaves?

- Integration of concepts. Are the children using ideas about fall and leaves in their art, play, and other creations, without prompting, in a way that demonstrates understanding?

WORD BANK

autumn, conifer, deciduous, fall, float, rustling, season, twirl

STEM SKILLS

Communication, Creativity, Data Analysis (graphing leaf collection), Investigation, Problem Solving (engineering a tree), Technology Use (making leaf press)

OVERVIEW

Children explore the signs of autumn and play with falling, changing, and dancing leaves.

BACKGROUND FOR ADULTS

Fall is the transition time from summer to winter. On or around June 21, the summer solstice in the Northern Hemisphere, we experience the longest day of the year. After June 21, the length of each day slowly decreases. On the autumnal equinox (September 22 or 23), the hours of daylight and night are equal. Throughout fall, the daylight continues to decrease each day until the winter solstice (December 21 or 22), the shortest day of the year.

As winter approaches in temperate regions, animals begin to prepare for the cold. Some migrate to warmer areas where there is more food, whereas others gather food or add an extra layer of fat to store energy or extra fur to keep warm.

The colder temperatures and shorter days also trigger responses in deciduous trees and other plants. Chlorophyll, the green pigment in leaves, starts to break down, revealing yellow or orange pigments that were concealed by the green chlorophyll. Red pigments are not usually present in leaves during summer, but they form when temperatures drop and photosynthesis slows. Through this process, deciduous tree leaves change color in the autumn. Meanwhile, the cells at the base of

did you know?

Forest Fact

Fallen leaves are an essential part of a forest's ecosystem. The fallen "leaf litter" shields the soil from hard rains, holding in moisture and preventing erosion. It also protects tree seeds that will germinate the following spring. Nutrients that leach from the dead leaves nourish the seedlings.

INTRODUCING THE THEME

Ask children, "What does your family do in the autumn to get ready for winter? Have you changed the clothes that you wear? How? As the temperature gets cooler, how are the animals and plants changing?"

each leaf stem begin to die, forming a barrier that keeps water and nutrients from traveling into the leaf. When the attachment breaks, the leaf falls to the ground.

Unlike deciduous trees, conifer trees do not lose all their leaves in fall. They often have small, thin needles with a waxy coating that prevents freezing and water loss during winter. The small surface area of the needles also reduces the amount of snow that can accumulate on them, decreasing the potential for them to break off. Conifer branches are also more flexible than their deciduous counterparts, which prevents them from breaking under heavy snow. They simply bend down at an angle under the weight of snow until the snow slides off to the ground.

Research suggests that the timing and duration of deciduous trees' fall color is shifting due to the changing climate. Warmer temperatures tend to delay the onset of peak colors and also make them disappear sooner, leading to a shorter fall foliage season.

Investigations into signs of autumn can lead children to ask questions about weather, the length of days, seeds, animals preparing for winter, trees that don't lose their leaves, and endless other possibilities. Get outside and enjoy the show while it lasts!

FEATURED EXPERIENCE: Autumn Adventure

Materials: Collection bags or small pails for each child, paint samples, magnifying lenses

Begin with taking an excursion around the play yard or neighborhood when leaves are falling. On the way, collect fallen leaves, seeds, nuts, and fruits for use in art projects, games, and science investigations. Watch for leaves beginning to change color, and try to match fallen leaves to the leaves still on the trees.

Find an appropriate place to stop and dig in the leaf litter under a tree. Try to find evidence of last year's leaves. You might find very small bits of leaves, leaf stems, or leaf skeletons. Talk about how leaves break down into smaller and smaller pieces until they become part of the soil.

Continue your excursion, noticing changes in the temperature by looking for frost on the grass and noting whether you can see your breath. Observe animals preparing for cooler temperatures, including squirrels collecting nuts, insects searching for places to spend the winter, and birds migrating south. Listen to the sounds feet or wheels make as you move through leaves or on frosty grass.

Back inside, encourage the children to examine the leaves you collected with magnifying lenses. Ask them questions like, "What colors do you see in the leaves? Which is your favorite color? When you touch the leaves, how do they feel? Which leaf feels the most interesting to you? Why do you think leaves fall off the trees? Show me some leaves that have tears or holes in them. What do you think happened to those leaves? What will happen to the leaves now that they are on the ground?"

You can also try comparing paint sample cards with the colors found in nature on your autumn adventure. Be sure to read the names of the paint colors as you hand them out—the names are great vocabulary boosters!

 SAFETY! For safety information and other ideas for conducting learning outdoors, see Appendix G: Tips for Outdoor Learning.

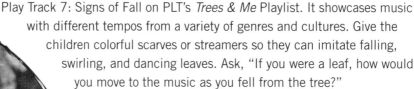 

GROUP EXPERIENCES

Music and Movement

3 **PRETEND TO BE DANCING LEAVES**

Materials: Fall-colored scarves or streamers, Track 7 on PLT's *Trees & Me* Playlist (scan QR code)

Play Track 7: Signs of Fall on PLT's *Trees & Me* Playlist. It showcases music with different tempos from a variety of genres and cultures. Give the children colorful scarves or streamers so they can imitate falling, swirling, and dancing leaves. Ask, "If you were a leaf, how would you move to the music as you fell from the tree?"

After the dance, invite the children to talk about how they felt dancing to the music. Leave out the props and music for the children to continue the experience.

SING A FALL SONG

Take the children outside, teach them this simple song, and enjoy the actions together. Change the last line to include other ways that leaves move (e.g., dance, float, soar, tumble, twirl).

> **Hanging on the Tree**
> Tune: Ring Around the Rosy
>
> Hangin' on the tree-ee.
> Winter's coming—whee-ee!
> Autumn, Autumn,
> We all fall down!

Reading and Writing

READ A STORY AND WRITE A BOOK

Materials: *Leaf Man* by Lois Ehlert, pressed leaves, book-making supplies

Read *Leaf Man* by Lois Ehlert. Talk about writing a group book that is about a leaf person or animal. Together, decide who or what the book will be about and what will happen in the story. Children can illustrate the story using leaves they collected on walks or at their homes. Press the leaves in leaf presses (see Woodworking), or place them in between the pages of a book. Then glue the leaves to paper, and make a group book.

Enjoying Snacks Together

HIDE-AND-SEEK SNACK

Recipe: Trail mix (oat cereal, popcorn, pretzels, chocolate candies or chips, raisins, etc.), containers (small reusable snack containers, wax paper bags, or zip-top bags)

 Before snack time, prepare individual servings of trail mix for each child in your group. Hide the containers outside. Ask, "If you are hungry, where do you look for food? If you were an animal and you didn't have a kitchen or grocery store, where would you find your food?"

Tell the children that they are going to pretend to be hungry squirrels. Ask, "What kinds of food have you seen squirrels eating? Where do squirrels find their food?"

Take the children to the area where the snacks are hidden. Tell them that as soon as they find one hidden snack, they should bring it back to where you are standing and wait while the others find their snacks.

⚠ **SAFETY!** Be aware of any food allergies, dietary needs, or choking hazards for the children in your group.

FREE EXPLORATION

Art

CREATE DRIED LEAF ART

Materials: Glue, tagboard, crushed or dried leaves, glitter, sand, soil, mixing bowls

Add dried leaves, glitter, sand, soil, and bowls for mixing. Invite the children to crumble the leaves and to mix them with the other items. Show the children how to paint designs with glue on heavy tagboard and to sprinkle the designs with the dried leaf mixtures.

EXPERIMENT WITH LEAF STENCILS

Provide leaf stencils for embossing, splatter painting, stenciling, or tracing. Offer paints in basic fall colors (red, orange, yellow, green), and encourage mixing and blending to create the subtle shades of color that make autumn beautiful.

🌲 Outdoor Play

Try these fun outdoor fall activities:

- **(3)** Provide rakes and leaf bags or large baskets for leaf play. (With younger children, show them how to scoop up leaves with their hands and toss them in the air.) While you work, sing Autumn Leaves Are Falling Down!

  ### Autumn Leaves Are Falling Down!
  Tune: London Bridge Is Falling Down

  Autumn leaves are falling down,
  Falling down, falling down.
  Autumn leaves are falling down,
  Red. Yellow. Brown.
  Take a rake and pile them up,
  Pile them up, pile them up.
  Take a rake and pile them up,
  Red. Yellow. Brown.

- **(3)** Provide large pieces of fabric that the children can use as wings to fly around the play area. Mark North, South, East, and West on the sidewalk. As birds fly by, note the direction in which they are flying. Talk about why some birds need to fly south in winter so they can find food to eat.

- Place leaves on the sidewalk and spray them lightly with water from spray bottles to create leaf prints on the sidewalk. Provide large sheets of paper and crayons for making leaf and bark rubbings outdoors.

- Provide sheets of acetate, plastic wrap, or cellophane wrapping paper in fall colors. Encourage the children to play with colors by looking through various see-through layers.

Take It Outside!

Have the children lie under a tree and watch leaves falling. Ask the children, "Does a leaf fall straight down, or do some leaves move through the air in different ways? How does the wind change the way they fall?" To end the activity, have the children try to catch the falling leaves.

Discovery Table

LOOK INSIDE NUTS

Provide tree nuts, hammers, magnifying lenses, nut crackers, and safety glasses to crack open nuts and see what is inside.

 SAFETY! Be aware of any allergies and choking hazards for the children in your group.

⚙ ENGINEER A TREE

Challenge children to engineer a free-standing "tree" using craft sticks, play dough, and leaves (craft or real). Point out that there is no wrong or right way to construct the tree, but it should be able to stand on its own when finished. (See Appendix D: Career Exploration and STEM Skills for information about developing career skills.)

Math and Manipulatives

 GRAPH A LEAF COLLECTION

Make a simple graph on a sheet of paper. Glue leaves (or leaf cut-outs) of different colors down the left side of the paper. Next to each leaf, the children can glue leaves of the same color. Total each row. Try the same activity with leaves of different sizes or shapes. See Appendix H: Bringing Nature Inside for more information about using natural objects in learning activities.

WORK WITH TREE SEEDS

Collect a large variety of tree seeds (e.g., acorns, basswood seeds, buckeyes, hickory nuts, maple pods, sycamore seeds, walnuts). Use the seeds for counting, measuring, sorting, and weighing activities. Make a set of paper plates numbered from 1 to 10. For younger children, use fewer numbers and put dots on the plate to represent each number. Encourage the children to put the plates in order and to count out the number of seeds indicated on each plate. Younger children can place a seed on each dot.

⚠ **SAFETY!** Be aware of any allergies or choking hazards for the children in your group.

Woodworking

 MAKE LEAF PRESSES

For each press, provide two 8- by 8-inch pieces of wood (¼-inch plywood works well) with holes drilled in the corners, four 3-inch-long bolts with wing nuts, 6- by 6-inch pieces of cardboard, and 6- by 6-inch pieces of newsprint or absorbent scrap paper. Encourage the children to sand the boards and assemble the presses. They can press leaves for use in games and art projects. For more information, see Appendix I: Woodworking for Everyone.

Explore Careers

Invite children to explore a green job that involves being outside in the fall—
GARDENER. A gardener is someone who cares for trees and other plants in outdoor spaces. Encourage children to be gardeners by doing simple fall garden tasks. They might pick up sticks or rake leaves that have fallen to the ground, help clean up vegetable beds, or plant spring-blooming bulbs.

GARDENER

EARLY LEARNING STANDARDS

SCIENCE

Practices
- Asking questions and defining problems
- Developing and using models
- Planning and carrying out investigations
- Using mathematics and computational thinking

Concepts
- Biodiversity and humans
- Structure and function
- Weather and climate

ENGLISH LANGUAGE ARTS

Practices
- Speaking and listening: comprehension and collaboration

Concepts
- Speaking and listening: presentation of knowledge and ideas
- Reading: key ideas and details
- Writing: text types and purpose

MATH

Practices
- Reason abstractly and quantitatively

Concepts
- Counting and cardinality
- Measurement and data

SOCIAL STUDIES

Concepts
- Geography: geographic representations

READING IS FUN!

Ehlert, Lois. *Leaf Man.* **Boston: Harcourt Children's Books, 2005.** With a body made of fallen leaves and acorns for eyes, Leaf Man takes off from a backyard and flutters away on the breeze, meandering past animals, over fields of fall vegetables, above waterways, and across prairie meadows. Ages 4–8. ISBN: 0152053042.

Hawk, Fran. *Count Down to Fall.* **Mount Pleasant, SC: Arbordale, 2013.** Counting backwards from 10, this book depicts colorful fall leaves, the trees from which they fall, and animals getting ready for winter. Ages 4–7. ISBN: 1934359947.

(3) **Henkes, Kevin.** *In the Middle of Fall.* **New York: Greenwillow Books, 2018.** This board book introduces the unique beauty of the fall season. Watch the world transform as a gust of wind turns the whole world to yellow, red, and orange. Ages 1–4. ISBN: 0062747266.

Muth, Jon J. *Hi, Koo!: Year of Seasons.* **New York: Scholastic, 2014.** Join a panda named Koo and two human siblings as they help to stretch the imagination with 26 haikus about the four seasons. Ages 4–7. ISBN: 0545166683.

Pak, Kenard. *Goodbye Autumn, Hello Winter.* **New York: Holt, 2017.** A brother and sister explore nature and stroll through their town, saying goodbye to autumn and welcoming the first snow of winter. Ages 3–6. ISBN: 1627794166.

Sayre, April Pulley. *Trout Are Made of Trees.* **Watertown, MA: Charlesbridge, 2008.** Two young children and their dads find out how a leaf can become a fish, as they observe life in and around a stream. Ages 4–8. ISBN: 1580891381.

Fall for Trees

Things to Do Together

We are exploring autumn and all the changes that happen to trees and plants at this time of the year. Here are some activities you and your child can do together:

- Collect and press one leaf from each tree in your yard, along your street, or in a neighborhood park.

- Pick apples or other tree fruits at an orchard, or visit a farmers' market.

- Eat tree fruits such as apples, oranges, mangoes, and pears.

- Bake an apple pie.

- Read stories about autumn.

- Send pictures of colorful autumn leaves to friends and family who live in places without fall color. If you live in an area with little fall color, ask friends and family to send pictures of leaves to you!

→ Family, Friends, and Forests: Talk about which forest trees you like better and why—ones that lose their leaves each year or ones that stay green all year.

 **Do Your Part**

Participate in a fall harvest at a neighborhood community garden or orchard. Donate some of the harvest to a local food pantry to help others in need. See **ampleharvest.org** to search for food pantries in your area that take garden-fresh food donations.

Help build your child's vocabulary by using some of these new words in your conversations:

_____

_____

_____

We are reading the following books. Check them out from your library, and invite your child to share them with you.

_____

_____

_____

Evergreens in Winter

OBJECTIVES

Provide opportunities and materials for children to:

- Observe seasonal changes in nature.
- Compare the cones, leaves, and twigs of different evergreen trees.
- Practice fine motor skills while making treats for wildlife in winter.
- Write an imaginative story about animals finding their treats.
- Express feelings about winter through music, movement, and art.
- Incorporate the knowledge they gain into their everyday world.
- Play outside in a natural setting.

ASSESSING THE EXPERIENCES

As you observe the children during the day, note the following:

- New vocabulary. In the children's conversations with you and one another, are they describing elements of winter?
- Questions about evergreens. Are the children asking questions that show an increased awareness of the variety of trees?
- New ideas. Are the children's experiences helping them form new ideas or refine old ideas? Are they drawing new conclusions or asking new questions that are based on their observations?
- Integration of concepts. Are the children using ideas about evergreens or winter in their art, play, and other creations, without prompting, in a way that demonstrates understanding?

WORD BANK

cone, conifer, deciduous, evergreen, needle, season, silhouette, spring, winter

STEM SKILLS

Collaboration (creating stories), Communication, Creativity, Investigation, Organization (sorting cones), Problem Solving (designing a sled)

OVERVIEW

Children explore evergreen trees—and the season of winter—using their senses.

BACKGROUND FOR ADULTS

While several tree species stay green all winter in the southern and western United States (such as live oak and holly), these experiences will focus on conifers (like pines, spruces, firs, and hemlocks) that can be found across the country and that stay green all year round. Conifers are trees that bear their seeds in cones and have needle-like or scalelike leaves.

Most conifers are evergreens. That means that while their needles do drop, it doesn't happen all at one time, so the trees remain green year-round.

AMAZING CONIFERS

Conifers are amazing plants with unique characteristics. All of the following can be found in the United States:

- Earth's tallest living thing: a coast redwood
- Earth's largest living thing: a giant sequoia
- Earth's oldest living thing: a Great Basin bristlecone pine

did you know?

Forest Fact

Evergreen trees often have needle-shaped or waxy coated leaves. These features prevent water loss and help the trees survive winter cold.

INTRODUCING THE THEME

Materials: Twigs and leaves from evergreen and deciduous trees

Display a variety of twigs from evergreen trees and deciduous trees. Invite children to smell them; scratch the twigs and smell them again; and feel the leaves of the evergreens. Ask, "Which twigs do you like best? How are the leaves the same? How are they different? How are the leaves of evergreen trees different from the leaves of trees that lose their leaves in fall?"

Conifers growing in the northern United States and in Canada have special adaptations that help them survive the cold temperatures and heavy snows of winter. These characteristics include:

- Triangular shapes that shed snow

- Narrow, wax-covered leaves that help trees retain moisture

- Sap that contains a chemical similar to "antifreeze" that keeps trees from freezing

A changing climate is likely to cause changes in our conifer forests. Research suggests that the pine-juniper woodlands of the southwestern United States may decline by the end of this century due to rising temperatures. However, research also shows that sustainable forest management in conifer forests of the northeastern United States can increase the amount of carbon stored in trees, helping to reduce carbon dioxide in the atmosphere and mitigate the effects of climate change.

Evergreen trees are just one of the wonders of winter. Enjoy exploring these greens!

FEATURED EXPERIENCE: Winter Treats

Materials: A book about animals in winter (see Reading Is Fun! for suggestions), yarn or string, large pinecones, peanut butter, cornmeal

Read a book about animals in winter, such as *Over and Under the Snow* by Kate Messner. Ask, "What animals have you seen in winter? What other animals do you think live nearby? Have you ever put out food for birds or other animals at your house? What do you think might happen if we put out food for birds?"

Invite the children to make pinecone feeders for birds. First, they should use the yarn to tie a loop around the pinecone so they can hang the treat from a tree. Mix one part peanut butter with five parts cornmeal and pack the mixture into the crevices of the pinecone. This Audubon-approved all-season mixture will attract woodpeckers, chickadees, titmice, and warblers.

 Head outside! Allow children to decide where to place their pinecones, such as in an evergreen tree, on a fence, or on the ground. If possible, try to place some of them where they can be seen from a window. Visit the pinecones as often as possible. Ask, "Who do you think ate the food? Did they leave any clues? Why do you think the treats on the _____ disappeared before the treats on the _____?"

Note: You may want to check first that it's okay to have birdfeeders in your setting. Be sure to replace or remove pinecone feeders after a couple of weeks.

 SAFETY! Be aware of any food allergies or choking hazards for the children in your group.

PROJECT LEARNING TREE®

Music and Movement

MAKE TREE SILHOUETTES

Materials: Bright light (flashlight, projector light), blank wall or large sheet, copy of Tree Shapes template in Appendix J: Ready-to-Go Resources

After spending time outdoors observing different tree shapes, shine a bright light on a blank wall or large sheet. Encourage the children to take turns creating tree silhouettes by using their bodies. Show the Tree Shapes template, which gives some examples of silhouettes. Ask, "How can you make your body look like a tree that loses its leaves? How can you make your body look like an oak tree? A spruce tree?"

Reading and Writing

CREATE AND SHARE WINTER STORIES

After the children make pinecone feeders (see Featured Experience), invite them to think about which animals might eat their treats. Encourage them to write or dictate a short story about what will happen when the animals find their treats. Assemble the individual pages into a group book, or post them on the bulletin board. Storytelling can be an effective way to engage a range of learners. For more suggestions, see Appendix B: Diverse Learners, Diverse Needs.

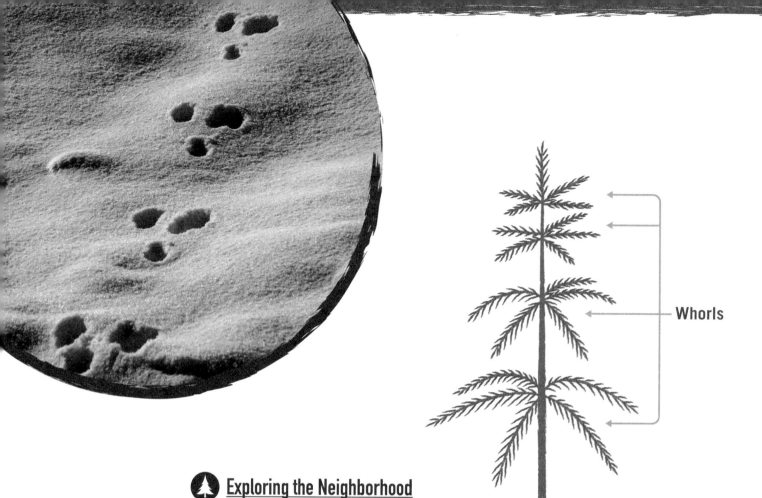

Whorls

🌲 Exploring the Neighborhood

As you explore the neighborhood in winter:

- Look for knobs and weird branches on deciduous trees. With the leaves gone, the shapes are easier to see.

- Search for animal homes in deciduous trees. Nests and holes should be more visible now than in summer.

- Search on the ground for tracks and other signs of animals.

- **③** Stop and listen to the sounds of winter (e.g., wind or snow under feet). Ask, "How does our walk sound, smell, or look different from the last time we walked? What is the same?"

- Find places that are out of the wind (e.g., close to a building, or next to or under a tree or hedge). Ask, "If you were an animal outside in winter, where would you stay?"

- **③** Search on the ground for cones. Look up high in the trees for cones still on the trees. Some trees hold their cones for more than a year.

- Plan to visit the trees again in the spring to look for new growth on the tips of the branches.

- Lie down under evergreens and look up through the branches. Talk about the patterns you see. Experience the way evergreens provide shelter from wind, rain, and snow.

- Look for the whorls of branches on conifers, such as pine, spruce, and fir. Each year, the tree adds a new whorl of branches. You can estimate the age of the tree by counting the whorls. Add two or three years to represent the first few years of growth before the tree started making whorls.

⚠️ **SAFETY!** For safety information and other ideas for conducting learning outdoors, see Appendix G: Tips for Outdoor Learning.

Enjoying Snacks Together

EAT EVERGREEN TREE SANDWICHES

Recipe: Plastic knives and plates; whole-grain bread; softened cream cheese tinted with green food coloring; cranberries, dates, figs, nuts, raisins, sunflower seeds, or other dried fruits; hot drinks

Using plastic knives, show children how to cut bread into triangles, spread them with cream cheese, and decorate them with nuts, seeds, or dried fruits. Serve the tree snacks with hot drinks made from trees (e.g., cocoa or tea, such as wintergreen, birch, or safrole-free sassafras).

 SAFETY! Be aware of any food allergies, dietary needs, or choking hazards for the children in your group.

FREE EXPLORATION

Art

PAINT WITH EVERGREEN PAINTBRUSHES

Materials: Evergreen needles, tape, paints, paper

Invite the children to dip small spruce branches into paint and to swirl them on large pieces of paper. Gather several pine needles into a bundle and wrap them with tape to form a brush that you can use for large paintings. Or use one pine needle for delicate paintings. Press cedar sprigs onto paint pads, then onto paper, to make prints.

Outdoor Play

Try these fun outdoor winter activities:

- Make evergreen angels (instead of snow angels) in a bed of fallen needles.
- Make a snow shelter, or build a shelter out of discarded Christmas tree boughs.
- Find evergreens outside and "hide" under them like animals would.
- Use child-size shovels to clear sidewalks or play areas. Haul away snow using sleds.
- Spread evergreen boughs cut from discarded Christmas trees over garden areas and flowerbeds after the ground freezes to protect the plants from extreme temperature changes.
- Use diluted food coloring in spray bottles to color the snow.
- On a sunny day, stand like trees and trace silhouettes on the sidewalk with chalk.
- Look for signs of animals (e.g., tracks, droppings, feathers, fur).

Take It Outside!

3 Try painting with snow on a tree trunk or fence (the texture will grip the snow). Show children how to make designs with handfuls of snow. If the snow is wet enough, they can even throw snowballs at the fence to make a picture. If there's no snow, children can use water.

Discovery Table

MAKE A SNOWY FOREST

Collect snow and place it in tubs or on a table with raised sides. Provide evergreen twigs and branches and invite children to stick them into the snow to make their own forest. (Alternatively, children could do this outside in a real snowbank.)

FEEL PRICKLY AND TICKLY BRANCHES

Encourage the children to bring in small sprigs from evergreens in their yards or from their Christmas trees. Label boxes "prickly" and "tickly" so the children can sort the branches. Provide magnifying lenses so they can explore the different shapes of leaves. Challenge the children to find as many different kinds of evergreens as possible.

⚙ DESIGN A MINI-SLED

For an engineering challenge, encourage children to build a "mini-sled" that will slide down a slope. Provide materials such as 6" x 8" pieces of cardboard, coffee filters, plastic sheeting, felt, straws, tape, and glue, as well as pennies or washers for weights. You may want to point out that paper and cardboard are often made from evergreen trees. To test out the sleds, hold a race down a snowy slope, playground slide, or board propped against a table.

Math and Manipulatives

 SORT CONES

Using cones collected on walks, from home, or purchased, invite the children to sort the cones by size, shape, weight, or kind. Make graphs to show how many of each shape or kind the children have found. Younger children can simply sort them into boxes labeled "big" and "little."

Dramatic Play

 PRETEND TO BE ANIMALS

Set up an artificial evergreen tree in a play area. Provide animal puppets for the children to use as they pretend to be animals staying warm in and under the evergreen tree. Provide a variety of food (e.g., pretend corn, fruits, nuts) so they can search for something to eat. The following traditional nursery rhyme is an example of an animal scene children can portray.

High in the Pine Tree

High in the pine tree,
The little mourning dove
Made a little nursery
To please her little love.

"Coo," said the mourning dove,
"Coo," said she
In the long, shady branches
Of the dark pine tree.

Woodworking

MAKE WOOD BLOCKS

Saw pine or spruce lumber into natural blocks to use in activities. Sand them smooth. For more information, see Appendix I: Woodworking for Everyone.

Explore Careers

Invite children to explore a green job that involves evergreen trees—**TREE FARMER**. These farmers plant and grow the trees that people use for the winter holidays. Provide crayons, paper, and markers to draw evergreen trees. Children can then practice "pruning" their trees by cutting them out! (As children are developing their skill with scissors, be sure to monitor scissor work.)

TREE FARMER

EARLY LEARNING STANDARDS

SCIENCE

Practices
- Asking questions and defining problems
- Developing and using models

Concepts
- Biodiversity and humans
- Organization for matter and energy flow in organisms
- Structure and function
- Weather and climate

ENGLISH LANGUAGE ARTS

Practices
- Speaking and listening: comprehension and collaboration

Concepts
- Speaking and listening: presentation of knowledge and ideas
- Reading: key ideas and details

MATH

Concepts
- Measurement and data

SOCIAL STUDIES

Concepts
- Geography: geographic representations

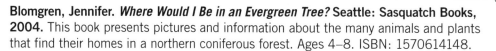

READING IS FUN!

Blomgren, Jennifer. *Where Would I Be in an Evergreen Tree?* **Seattle: Sasquatch Books, 2004.** This book presents pictures and information about the many animals and plants that find their homes in a northern coniferous forest. Ages 4–8. ISBN: 1570614148.

Hall, Kirsten. *Snow Birds.* **New York: Abrams Books, 2020.** Through rhyming verse and striking illustrations, this book celebrates the resourceful birds who persevere through winter's snowy weather and freezing temperatures. Ages 4–8. ISBN: 1419742035.

Messner, Kate. *Over and Under the Snow.* **San Francisco: Chronicle Books, 2011.** Over the snow, the world is hushed and white, but under the snow is a secret world of squirrels and snowshoe hares, bears and bullfrogs, and many others living outside during the winter. Ages 5–8. ISBN: 0811867846.

(3) Priddy, Richard. *Bright Baby Touch and Feel Winter.* **New York: St. Martin's Publishing Group, 2011.** This delightful board book invites babies and toddlers to explore the magical sights and textures of winter, including a sparkling snowflake and a winter forest. Ages 1-3. ISBN: 0312509766.

Taylor, Sean, and Alex Morss. *Winter Sleep: A Hibernation Story.* **London: words & pictures, 2019.** Follow a child and his grandma through a winter landscape to explore how the Earth goes to sleep for winter. Ages 5–7. ISBN: 0711242844.

Yee, Wong Herbert. *Tracks in the Snow.* **New York: Square Fish, 2007.** In this celebration of snow and winter, a little girl follows tracks outside her window after a fresh snowfall, only to discover that they are hers from the day before. Ages 2–6. ISBN: 0312371349.

Yolen, Jane. *Owl Moon.* **New York: Penguin Group (USA), 1987.** A girl and her father go owling on a moonlit winter night near the farm where they live. Learn about what they see and hear hidden in ink-blue shadows. Ages 3–8. ISBN: 0399214577.

Evergreens in Winter

Things to Do Together

We are exploring evergreen trees and the winter season. Here are some activities you and your child can do together:

- Search for evergreen-scented items in your home (e.g., air fresheners, car fresheners, cleaners, deodorants). Talk about why you like or don't like the smell.

- Take a walk through an evergreen forest. Look for ways that evergreens provide protection from wind, rain, and snow.

- Bundle up and enjoy an early evening stroll around your yard, neighborhood, or nearby park. Look for ways that animals survive in winter.

- Enjoy a fun wintertime activity together, like making a wreath from evergreens or going sledding.

- Enjoy some hot tea or cocoa.

→ **Family, Friends, and Forests:** Talk about what it might be like to sleep all winter, like some forest animals do.

 **Do Your Part**

Bring winter cheer to people in a senior center or assisted living facility by donating children's drawings of evergreen trees or other nature scenes. Call ahead to be sure the facility can accept your donation.

Help build your child's vocabulary by using some of these new words in your conversations:

_____

_____

_____

_____

We are reading the following books. Check them out from your library, and invite your child to share them with you.

_____

_____

_____

Best Buds

OBJECTIVES

Provide opportunities and materials for children to:

- Observe seasonal changes in nature, especially the new growth of trees.
- Experiment with twigs, buds, flowers, and seeds.
- Describe spring using words that imitate sounds.
- Express feelings about spring through music, movement, and art.
- Incorporate the knowledge they gain into their everyday world.
- Play outside in a natural setting.

ASSESSING THE EXPERIENCES

As you observe the children during the day, note the following:

- New vocabulary. In the children's conversations with you and one another, are they using more terms that describe trees, buds, flowers, and spring?
- Questions about trees and spring. Are the children asking questions about these topics?
- New ideas. Are the children's experiences helping them form new ideas or refine old ideas? Are they pointing out new growth or noticing changes in the environment?
- Integration of concepts. Are the children using the ideas of trees and spring in their art, play, and other creations, without prompting, in a way that demonstrates understanding?

WORD BANK

bloom, blossom, branch, bud, calendar, growing, leaf, pattern, season, spring, twig

STEM SKILLS

Communication, Creativity, Investigation, Organization (comparing twigs), Problem Solving (building nests, under Outdoor Play)

OVERVIEW

Children explore twigs, buds, and tree flowers while they celebrate the coming of spring.

BACKGROUND FOR ADULTS

When does spring arrive? The signs of spring come to different areas of the country at different times. The return of certain migratory birds, the smell of the soil, and the blooming of the first flowers are all indicators of spring. For some places, these signs appear before March 1. In other places, the ground is still frozen in April!

Wherever you live in North America, the days become longer than the nights starting at the spring equinox (around March 20) and continue to lengthen until the summer solstice (around June 21). During this time, the sun appears higher in the sky every day. The days become steadily warmer as the sun's rays hit the Earth more directly and for a longer time each day.

One sure sign of spring is the appearance of new leaves and flowers on trees and shrubs. When a deciduous tree's leaves drop in the fall, its leaves for the next spring are already forming. The immature leaves, stems, and sometimes even flowers are located on the twigs in packages called buds. The buds are made of tough scales that form a waterproof case around these immature tree parts. In spring, the scales fall off the buds, and the leaves, stems, and flowers begin to unfurl and grow.

did you know?

Forest Fact

In preparation for winter, trees in temperate climates, such as box elder, form resting leaf buds that are resistant to frost. They remain dormant all winter long. In spring, as the sun gets brighter and the days get longer, sunlight triggers the buds to burst open.

INTRODUCING THE THEME

Materials: Twigs from deciduous and evergreen trees, bulbs (flower or onion), seed packets (flower or garden), tree seeds (acorns, maple seeds, or nuts)

Display a variety of plant materials (e.g., twigs, bulbs, flowers, seeds). There should be one item for each child. Pass the plant materials around and look at them closely. Talk about spring and how plants change and grow during this time. Ask, "Do you think any of these things can grow and change? What do you think will happen if we put this twig in water? What do you think will happen if we plant this seed in soil?"

Plants and animals don't look at a calendar to note when spring begins. They take their clues from the lengthening days and increasing temperatures. Buds on trees and shrubs that are not native to an area might open before native plants because their time clocks are set differently. You might also notice that trees and plants on the south sides of buildings or other protected places develop their leaves sooner than other trees do. In addition, our changing climate is causing spring to arrive earlier in many places than it used to, due to increasing global temperatures.

The seasonal changes of springtime affect people, too. The increased sunlight causes changes in our hormonal and metabolic functions, helping us feel more hopeful and resilient. Spending time outside in warm, sunny spring weather can also lead to higher mood and better memory.

Enjoy the spring!

FEATURED EXPERIENCE: Talk to the Trees

Materials: Picture book about trees in spring (optional, see Reading Is Fun! for suggestions)

If possible, read a picture book about trees in spring, such as *It's Spring!* by Linda Glaser or *Trees in Spring* by Jenny Fretland VanVoorst. Ask children to describe the changes to trees and other living things that happen in spring and that are depicted in the book.

Talk about what is happening to the trees in your neighborhood. Ask, "Do any of our trees have new leaves or flowers? What have you seen? Do you think what happened to the trees in the book is happening to the trees in our neighborhood? Why or why not? If you could talk to a tree—or ask it any question—what would you say to the tree about these changes?"

 Head outside to explore trees. Model going right up to the trees and talking to them. Select some trees that haven't leafed out yet. If you know what kind of tree you are looking at, address it by name. If you don't know, give it a name (e.g., "Good morning, Tall Tree with Rough Bark!"). Point out the things you think are unusual, beautiful, or remarkable about each tree you visit. Invite the children to talk to the trees, too.

While you are outside, watch for other signs of spring. Older children might enjoy making a map of the trees in their neighborhood.

⚠️ **SAFETY!** For safety information and other ideas for conducting learning outdoors, see Appendix G: Tips for Outdoor Learning.

PROJECT LEARNING TREE®

GROUP EXPERIENCES

Music and Movement

 DANCE AROUND A MAYPOLE

Materials: Pole or tree with 6–8 feet of unbranched trunk, eight 16-foot ribbons or strips of fabric, jingle bells and garlands (optional), Track 8 on PLT's *Trees & Me* Playlist (scan QR code at right)

People in many European countries celebrate the end of winter and welcome spring by dancing around a maypole. Although maypole dances are usually held on May 1, pick any warm, sunny day for your dance.

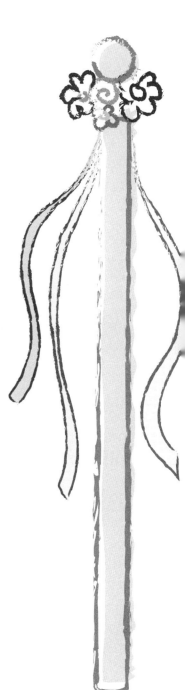

A traditional maypole is a tall sapling secured in the ground. You can use a flagpole, a tall young tree, or even a broomstick. Tie one ribbon on the pole for each dancer. Limit the number of dancers to eight at a time and repeat the dance described below as many times as necessary. Any children who are not dancing can play rhythm instruments to add to the music. Make the dance as festive as possible by asking the children to wear bright-colored clothes, tying jingle bells on their ankles, putting garlands of flowers or ivy on their heads, and allowing them to dance barefoot.

Dance to Track 8: Celtic Collection on PLT's *Trees & Me* Playlist, or sing the traditional folk song below to your own tune. First dance, skip, jump, and hop in one direction. Turn around and repeat to unwind the ribbons. Dance up to the pole and shout "Hello, Spring!" before backing away.

> **May Morning Dew**
>
> Summer is coming,
> oh, summer is near,
> With the leaves on the trees
> and the sky blue and clear.
> Small birds are singing
> their fond notes so true,
> And wildflowers are springing
> in the May morning dew.

After the dance, talk with the children about how the dance made them feel. Ask: "What parts of spring do you like the best? How can you show that you are happy about the warmer days and growing plants?"

PLAY PEEK-A-BOO WITH SPRING

Materials: 1 piece of brightly colored fabric per child,
Track 9 on PLT's *Trees & Me* Playlist (scan QR code at right)

Act out the arrival of spring by giving each child a brightly colored piece of fabric. Show the children how to stuff the fabric under their shirts or inside their jackets. Play Track 9: The Four Seasons—Spring by Vivaldi on PLT's *Trees & Me* Playlist. As the music builds, show the children how to let "spring" peek out from under their clothes and hide again. Tell them that when they think spring is ready, it can come out as fast or slow as it wants. Encourage them to let spring dance around. It can fly through the air, land softly on the ground, and brighten up the world.

Reading and Writing

DESCRIBE SPRING WITH SOUND

Talk about the arrival of spring. Ask, "How do you feel when you see flowers suddenly open up in spring? What colors do you notice in spring that you haven't seen all winter?" Invite the children to draw a picture of spring. When they are done, help them add words that describe how quickly trees, flowers, and lawns come to life in spring. Encourage the children to think of explosive words (e.g., bam, bang, boing, ka-boom, kapow, poof, pop, snap, whee, whoosh). Write their words next to flowers and leaves on the picture.

🌲 Exploring the Neighborhood

As you explore the neighborhood in spring:

- Look at trees in the distance. Sometimes you can see the tinge of green or yellow better on distant trees than on those close to you.

- Smell the soil after a spring rain.

- Look for sprouting grass, bulbs, and other plants.

- Listen for calling birds, frogs, and insects.

- Look for and smell tree flowers. Although a few trees have showy flowers, most are inconspicuous. Tree flowers have different smells, some very fragrant and some without any odor at all.

- Feel the sun's warmth!

- Look for early-flowering bulbs in gardens. If possible, dig up a flowering bulb so the children can see where the plant stored its energy all winter. Replant the bulb with the children.

⚠️ **SAFETY!** For safety information and other ideas for conducting learning outdoors, see Appendix G: Tips for Outdoor Learning.

Enjoying Snacks Together

EAT SUNSHINE SANDWICHES

Recipe: English muffins, cream cheese, sunflower seeds, mandarin oranges (fresh or canned), plastic knives

 The children can make these sandwiches by spreading cream cheese on English muffins. They can put sunflower seeds in the center and can arrange mandarin orange sections around the outside to form the sun's rays. If you use canned oranges, drain them well. Take your "sunshine sandwiches" outside to eat in the sunshine!

⚠ **SAFETY!** Be aware of any food allergies, dietary needs, or choking hazards for the children in your group.

FREE EXPLORATION

Art

PAINT WITH PUSSY WILLOWS

Collect or purchase pussy willows and use them as brushes with watercolors or tempera paints. You can hot-glue a pussy willow bud on a pencil-size twig. The children will need to be gentle painters!

 DO ART OUTSIDE

Make outdoor easels by taping paper to the four sides of large cardboard boxes, on fences, or on trees. Take out paints, brushes, and water cups, and let nature inspire the children.

Take It Outside!

Provide stethoscopes or cups without bottoms for listening to trees. During early spring, you can hear tree sap moving up and down the trunk. The best time to listen is on a warm day that follows a cool night.

🌲 Outdoor Play

Try these fun outdoor spring activities:

- Provide pots, soil, and seeds so the children can plant in a small garden or in containers. Plants that grow quickly, like marigolds, peas, onion sets, and radishes, are good choices for eager gardeners.

- Pull up tree seedlings that have sprouted on the lawn, and plant them in pots.

- ⚙️ For an engineering challenge, encourage children to find nest-building materials in the play area (e.g., dried grass, leaves, mud, twigs) and to build bird or squirrel nests.

- Provide natural materials like cotton, jute, twine, or shredded wood or paper for the children to cut into short lengths (4–6 inches), and place around the play area. Put piles of small twigs and dry grass in open areas visible from indoors. Watch to see if the bits and pieces disappear over time. If you use bright colors, you might be lucky enough to see your "gifts" in neighborhood birds' nests.

- Turn over your compost pile.

- Look for nests in trees. They are easiest to see when the trees are bare.

- Invite the children to find twigs and turn them into magic wands. The children can gently touch things in nature and spread spring's magic. Be sure to explain that the magic won't take effect right away, but if they watch and wait, they'll see changes everywhere!

- **3** Have the children put on their rainboots and let them jump in puddles.

PROJECT LEARNING TREE®

Discovery Table

ENJOY A SNEAK PEEK OF SPRING

You can "force" some trees and shrubs to flower earlier by taking cuttings indoors. Apple, forsythia, willow, maple, oak, and pussy willows are good choices. Cut off small twigs with a sharp knife or pruner and put them in water immediately. Change the water frequently and recut the stem ends if needed. Compare the twigs with the trees and shrubs outside. Ask, "Which buds do you think will open first, the ones on the twigs we brought inside, or the ones on the twigs outside? Why? Which buds do you think will be flower buds? Which buds do you think have leaves inside them? Why do you think some trees have big flowers and some trees have little flowers?"

DISSECT BUDS

Collect fallen or pruned twigs that have large buds (e.g., buckeye, hickory, poplar, rhododendron, tulip tree, some viburnums). Using plastic knives, encourage the children to take the buds apart. Magnifying lenses will help them see the insides. Use a sharp knife to cut through a few buds and then put them in magnifying boxes.

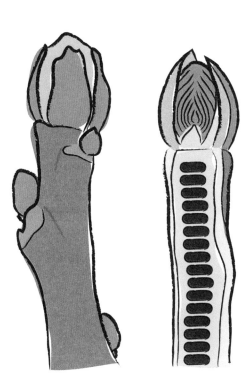

Math and Manipulatives

 ### COMPARE TWIGS

Use twigs collected on walks for counting, matching, sequencing, and sorting. Ask: "What are some things that are the same or different? Which twigs do you think came from the same kind of tree?" Encourage the children to sort the twigs by buds, color, or length. Ask, "How did you decide what to look at when you were sorting the twigs?"

Explore Careers

Invite children to explore a green job that involves the seasonal changes of plants—LANDSCAPE DESIGNER. Provide crayons and paper for children to be landscape designers, and draw their own creative landscape. Make a map for where trees, vegetables, or flowers could be planted in the yard, play yard, or local park. Consider designing a new space that will attract butterflies or promote quiet reflection. Spring is a great time to plant!

LANDSCAPE DESIGNER

EARLY LEARNING STANDARDS

SCIENCE

Practices
- Planning and carrying out investigations
- Analyzing and interpreting data

Concepts
- Patterns
- Scale, proportion, and quantity
- Stability and change
- Structure and function
- Systems and system models
- Weather and climate

ENGLISH LANGUAGE ARTS

Practices
- Speaking and listening: comprehension and collaboration

Concepts
- Speaking and listening: presentation of knowledge and ideas
- Reading: key ideas and details
- Writing: text types and purpose

MATH

Concepts
- Counting and cardinality

SOCIAL STUDIES

Concepts
- Geography: geographic representations
- Geography: human–environment interaction

READING IS FUN!

Butterworth, Chris. *The Things That I LOVE About Trees.* Somerville, MA: Candlewick, **2018.** Starting when trees are just getting their new buds in spring, this story follows the cycle of trees through the seasons. Ages 4–7. ISBN: 0763695696.

Florian, Douglas. *Handsprings: Poems and Paintings.* New York: Greenwillow Books, 2006. These 29 poems about spring are illustrated with watercolors and extol the many virtues of springtime. Ages 5–8. ISBN: 0060092807.

Glaser, Linda. *It's Spring!* Brookfield, CT: Millbrook Press, 2002. Simple text and bold paper sculpture convey the animal life, plant life, weather, and clothing, as well as the colors and feelings, associated with spring. Ages 4–8. ISBN: 0761313451.

(3) Henkes, Kevin. *When Spring Comes.* New York: Greenwillow Books, 2018. In this beautiful board book for young children, striking imagery, repetition, and alliteration introduce the transformation from quiet, cold winter to spring. Ages 1–4. ISBN: 0062741667.

(3) Lionni, Leo. *A Little Book About Spring.* New York: Random House, 2019. Discover the wonders of spring—from budding trees and chirping birds to croaking frogs—in this delightful board book. Ages 1–3. ISBN: 0062741667.

Stein, David. *Leaves.* New York: Putnam, 2007. A young bear cub tries to make sense of changing and falling leaves. He uses fallen leaves as bedding for a long winter's sleep, only to wake and find the tree has leafed out. Ages 2–5. ISBN: 0399246363.

VanVoorst, Jenny Fretland. *Trees in Spring.* Minneapolis: Jump!, 2016. Vibrant, full-color photos depict how trees respond to changes in spring by growing leaves and flowers. Ages 4–6. ISBN: 1620314819.

PROJECT LEARNING TREE®

Best Buds

Things to Do Together

We are exploring spring and all the changes that happen to trees and plants at this time of the year. Here are some activities you and your child can do together:

• Find a twig on a tree or shrub near your house. Tie a string around it so it is easy to find again. Take a picture of the twig every few days. Watch the buds swell and burst. Can you predict which buds will become flowers and which will become leaves?

• Watch carefully for tree flowers. Many tree flowers are small and easy to miss!

• Visit a wooded area, and look for the earliest flowers of spring.

• Start some flower or vegetable seeds indoors for transplanting into gardens or pots.

• Play in the mud! Splash in puddles! Take a walk in the rain!

→ Family, Friends, and Forests: Talk about changes to forests that come with spring.

Do Your Part

Volunteer at a spring clean-up event in a park or nature area in your community. Projects may include picking up trash, pulling weeds, or planting plants.

Help build your child's vocabulary by using some of these new words in your conversations:

_____

_____

_____

_____

We are reading the following books. Check them out from your library, and invite your child to share them with you.

_____

_____

_____

My Tree and Me

OBJECTIVES

Provide opportunities and materials for children to:

- Compare the bark, flowers, fruits, leaves, seeds, and twigs of different trees.
- Choose a favorite tree.
- Assemble a group scrapbook featuring favorite trees.
- Express feelings about trees through music, movement, and art.
- Incorporate the knowledge they gain into their everyday world.
- Play outside in a natural setting.

ASSESSING THE EXPERIENCES

As you observe the children during the day, note the following:

- New vocabulary. In the children's conversations with you and one another, are they using more terms about trees?
- Questions about trees. Are the children asking questions that show an increased awareness of tree diversity and features?
- New ideas. Are they able to express and explain their preferences?
- Integration of concepts. Are the children using trees or tree parts in their art, play, and other creations, without prompting, in a way that demonstrates understanding?

WORD BANK

adopt, bark, cone, favorite, flower, fruit, leaf, seed, special, twig

STEM SKILLS

Communication, Creativity, Data Analysis (labeling tree parts), Investigation, Organization (comparing trees), Problem Solving (creating tree maze), Technology Use (using rain gauge)

OVERVIEW

Children compare trees and identify distinguishing features.

BACKGROUND FOR ADULTS

Different kinds of trees vary in appearance, texture, and odor. Trees also come in different shapes, sizes, and colors—just like people. And just like people, every tree is special in some way. By seeing, touching, and smelling a diversity of trees, children can begin to understand and value the natural world around them. Here are just some of the characteristics that can set apart different trees.

Leaves: The shape of a leaf gives clues to a tree's identity. For example, willows have narrow leaves, cottonwoods have triangular leaves, firs have flat needles, and pines have round needles. Some leaves have "teeth," whereas others have lobes. Some leaves feel like sandpaper (slippery elm) and others look freshly waxed (magnolia).

Twigs and buds: Although many twigs and buds look alike, some stand out. Features like 2-inch-long thorns (hawthorn), buds shaped like onions (flowering dogwood), sticky buds (horse chestnut), and twigs with a distinct smell (balsam, black cherry, or yellow birch) help with tree identification.

did you know?

Forest Fact

One of the largest organisms ever discovered is a quaking aspen tree in southern Utah named "Pando." What looks like a large grove of trees is actually a single living organism, connected by a common root system. Pando is also the heaviest (13.2 million pounds) and oldest (several thousand years old) known living organism. Its roots cover an area the size of 80 football fields (108 acres)!

INTRODUCING THE THEME

Ask children, "Do you have a favorite tree? Where is your favorite tree located? Are there any special trees at your house, at your grandparents' house, on your street, or in your park? What makes a tree special to you?" Tell the children a story about a tree that is special to you.

Flowers, fruits, and seeds: Some people might choose their favorite tree based on the tree's flower or fruit. Some trees have showy flowers (tulip poplar), while others have distinctive seeds such as berries, winged seeds, nuts, pods, and cones.

Bark: Although many trees have similar bark, some trees have distinctive bark with unique characteristics. Shaggy bark (shagbark hickory), smooth white bark (paper birch), smooth gray bark (beech), and camouflage bark (sycamore) are just a few unique textures and colors that can differentiate trees.

Shape: For some trees, it is the shape that stands out. Some are pyramid-shaped, wider at the bottom than the top (spruce). Others are vase-shaped, wider at the top than the bottom (American elm). Some have upright branches that make a round shape (sugar maple), while others have a fountain shape (weeping willow).

By studying individual trees and taking a closer look at their bark, flowers, fruits, leaves, seeds, and twigs, children practice observation, classification, and identification skills.

FEATURED EXPERIENCE: Adopt a Favorite Tree

Materials: Cone, flag, or ribbon for each child; crayons and paper; digital camera; envelope or bag for each tree selected

 Go to a park or playground with several trees. Tell the children they are going to pick out a favorite tree to "adopt." As a group, visit several trees, noting their bark types, leaves, seeds, and shapes. Ask, "What do you like about this tree? How is this tree different from the other trees in this area? How will you decide which tree to choose?"

Give each child a cone, flag, or ribbon to mark his or her favorite tree. One at a time, visit the trees the children have marked, and invite the children to share why they made their choices. Encourage them to give the trees names. Using a digital camera, take pictures of the children and their favorite trees. Collect a leaf, seed, twig, flower, or combination of items from each tree chosen. Make a bark rubbing of the tree. Place the items from each tree in a large envelope, and label the envelope so you will remember which tree the parts came from. See the Reading and Writing section for ideas on how to use these parts.

Over the summer and during the other seasons, visit the trees as often as you can. These favorite or "adopted" trees can be the center for many of the experiences in this guide, thus helping to build a personal connection between the children and nature. Favorite trees are great places to read stories, celebrate birthdays, create art, play games, and relax. See also Appendix F: Traditional Knowledge and Gratitude Walk for another way to interact with adopted trees.

⚠ **SAFETY!** For safety information and other ideas for conducting learning outdoors, see Appendix G: Tips for Outdoor Learning.

Music and Movement

 3 **DANCE THE HOKEY POKEY**

On a sunny day, find a large tree standing alone. Ideally, you should be able to see the tree's entire shadow on the ground. Ask the children to find a place to stand where the sun meets the shade. Follow the leader around the edge of the shadow. Jump inside the shadow so that your bodies are in the shade. Jump out so that your bodies are in the sun. Now you are ready to dance the Hokey Pokey!

Hokey Pokey

You put your left leg in,
You put your left leg out,
You put your left leg in
And you shake it all about.
You do the Hokey Pokey,
and you turn yourself around,
And that's what it's all about…

SING AND DANCE WITH BILLY B

Play Track 10: Yummy, Yummy by Billy B on PLT's *Trees & Me* Playlist (scan QR code at right). Invite children to learn the lyrics and dance to the music. See Appendix C: *Trees & Me* Playlist for song lyrics and for tips on using this and other music selections.

Reading and Writing

MAKE AN *OUR FAVORITE TREES* SCRAPBOOK

After selecting favorite trees, read *Meeting Trees* by Scott Russell Sanders. Show children how to press the leaves they collected from their favorite trees. (See Woodworking in Activity 5: Fall for Trees for directions for making leaf presses, or simply place the leaves between the pages of large books.) Laminate the leaves, if desired. Use bark rubbings, leaves, photos, flowers, and seeds to make a digital or real scrapbook. For a digital book, scan or photograph the tree parts.

⚙ Encourage the children to draw pictures of their favorite trees, label the tree parts, and dictate stories about why their trees are special.

If they need help writing about their trees, suggest the following prompts:

- My tree's bark feels like _____.

- My tree is a home for _____.

- My tree is special because _____.

- When I'm sitting under my tree, I feel _____.

- When I'm next to my tree, I can see _____.

- In winter, spring, and fall, my tree looks different because _____.

PROJECT LEARNING TREE®

Enjoying Snacks Together

 PICNIC UNDER A TREE

Recipe: Lemonade (from concentrate or mix) or lemons, water, and sugar for making fresh lemonade, lemon juicer if needed, small chunks of frozen fruit

Make your own lemonade and serve it with small pieces of frozen fruit. While you eat and drink, ask the children how the frozen fruit feels in their mouths. Tell them that lemons grow on trees and ask what other tree fruits they like to eat and what other juices come from tree fruits.

⚠️ **SAFETY!** Be aware of any food allergies, dietary needs, or choking hazards for the children in your group.

FREE EXPLORATION

Art

FRAME YOUR FAVORITE TREE

Materials: Photograph of each child with his or her favorite tree, cardboard picture mats (inside opening equal to dimensions of photograph), natural objects (e.g., grass, leaves, seeds, twigs), glue

Provide picture mats and glue. Encourage the children to decorate the frames with natural objects they have collected. If possible, do this art activity outdoors where children are free to find natural objects to add to their frames as needed. Place a photograph of the child with his or her favorite tree in the frame.

POUND LEAF PICTURES

Materials: Hard wood surface, hammer with flat head, paper towels, paper or fabric for printing, variety of leaves

Gently hammering a leaf releases its chlorophyll and makes a print of the leaf on cloth or paper. Place a thick smooth board on the ground and place on top of it, in this order, a paper towel, the fabric or paper on which you want to print, a leaf, and another paper towel. Begin by pounding lightly to release the color without bursting the plant cells to pieces. Lift up a corner and peek at the impression. Continue hammering if necessary. Display the pictures on a bulletin board and out of direct sunlight.

Take It Outside!

Challenge children to guess which tree in the play yard, nearby park, or another area has the biggest trunk. Show them how to measure around each trunk using their outstretched hands and touching one another's fingertips to encircle the tree. You might graph their results by helping them make handprints on paper (with tempera paint) to show how many hands around each tree is.

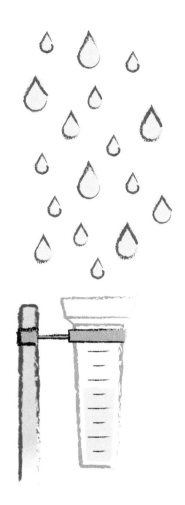

🌲 Outdoor Play

Try these fun outdoor activities related to trees:

- Play shadow tag by touching or "tagging" a shadow when a cue is called or the music stops.
- Make maple seed "rhino horn" noses, acorn cap whistles, and dandelion crowns. Think of ways to play with trees and plants!
- Put out a rain gauge and invite children to measure and monitor rainfall over the course of a week.
- During a dry time, water the trees in the play yard and along the sidewalk.
- Mulch the trees in your play yard.
- Do art outside on a comfortable day.
- **3** Stand by a tree and use your body to make the shape of the tree. Move on to the next tree and repeat.

Discovery Table

⚙ FAVORITE TREE MAZE

For an engineering challenge for older children, invite them to draw a small picture of a tree on a paper plate and create a maze that will move a marble around the plate and end up at the tree. Provide strips of paper, tape, wax craft sticks, and other craft supplies for creating their mazes. You might show children how they can create arches with the strips of paper and pathways with the wax craft sticks.

⚙ COMPARE AND LABEL SPECIAL TREES

Provide field guides and pressed leaves from the children's favorite trees. Encourage the children to compare the drawings in the field guides with the pressed leaves. As the trees are identified, post the leaves on a bulletin board and label them. Labels can be the common names of trees (e.g., redbud) or names the children have given them (e.g., heart-leaf tree).

Math and Manipulatives

PLAY A MEMORY GAME WITH LEAVES

Make two sets of pressed leaves mounted on card stock. Label one set with the trees' names, and laminate both sets. Encourage the children to sort and match the leaves or to play a game of "Memory" by themselves or with a friend.

HOW MANY CONES ARE YOU?

Provide cones from different trees, including both small and large cones. Encourage children to compare the length of their hands to the length of the cones. Which is longer? How many cones long are their arms? How many cones tall are they?

Explore Careers

Invite children to explore a green job that involves telling others about trees and other outdoor features—NATURE GUIDE. Make a loop of yarn or string and have children place it on the lawn or ground outside. They can pretend this is a teeny park that they can "walk" through with their fingers, imagining that small plants are trees, twigs are logs, and so on. Encourage them to be nature guides and give "tours" of their park, pointing out "trees," "logs," animals, rocks, and other features.

NATURE GUIDE

EARLY LEARNING STANDARDS

SCIENCE

Practices
- Asking questions and defining problems
- Analyzing and interpreting data
- Using mathematics and computational thinking

Concepts
- Interdisciplinary relationships in ecosystems
- Organization for matter and energy flow in organisms
- Patterns
- Scale, proportion, and quantity
- Stability and change
- Structure and function
- Systems and system models

ENGLISH LANGUAGE ARTS

Practices
- Speaking and listening: comprehension and collaboration

Concepts
- Speaking and listening: presentation of knowledge and ideas
- Writing: text types and purpose

MATH

Concepts
- Measurement and data

SOCIAL STUDIES

Concepts
- Geography: graphic representations
- Geography: human–environment interaction

READING IS FUN!

Baylor, Byrd. *Everybody Needs a Rock.* **New York: Aladdin, 1985.** In this delightful story, a child describes the 10 rules for finding your own personal rock. Ages 4–8. ISBN: 0689710518.

Boyd, Lizi. *Flashlight.* **San Francisco: Chronicle Books, 2014.** In this story without words, a child explores the woods after dark with a flashlight. Ages 3–6. ISBN: 1452118949.

Fredericks, Anthony D. *Tall Tall Tree: A Nature Book for Kids About Forest Habitats.* **Nevada City, CA: Dawn Publications, 2017.** High in a redwood tree, readers meet an unseen world of all kinds of animals and count them 1 to 10. Ages 3–8. ISBN: 1584696028.

Jones, Andrea Koehle. *The Wish Trees.* **Bloomington, IN: AuthorHouse, 2008.** Every child can help make the world a better place. In this book, children plant "wish trees" and discover the wonder of trees. Ages 3–5. ISBN: 1434392058.

(3) **Matheson, Christie.** *Tap the Magic Tree.* **New York: Greenwillow Books, 2016.** With this interactive board book, children tap, shake, jiggle, and even blow a kiss to help a lonely tree change through the seasons. Ages 1–3. ISBN: 0062274465.

Sanders, Scott Russell. *Meeting Trees.* **Bloomington, IN: Indiana University Press, 2018.** During a long walk through the forest with his father, a young boy discovers the wonders of nature as he learns about different kinds of trees and their special characteristics. Ages 4–8. ISBN: 0253034787.

Teckentrup, Britta. *Tree: A Peek-Through Picture Book.* **New York: Doubleday, 2016.** Through a hole in the book's cover, an owl invites readers inside to meet a tree and all its forest inhabitants during the changing seasons. Ages 3–6. ISBN: 1101932422.

PROJECT LEARNING TREE®

My Tree and Me

Things to Do Together

We are exploring our favorite trees! Here are some activities you and your child can do together:

- Find a special tree near your home to "adopt." Visit the tree whenever you can and observe how it changes. Take pictures if possible.

- Take care of the trees along your street. Dry spells during the summer are very stressful for trees. You can help them by giving them a good watering once a week during times of little or no rainfall.

- Go camping in a park, your backyard, or your own living room. To "camp" in your living room, you won't need any special equipment. Keep the lights out, sing songs, and tell stories. Your child might like to sleep in a sleeping bag or nest of blankets on the floor, or in a tent made of blankets draped over a chair.

- Have a summer picnic under a tree.

- Enjoy outdoor summer activities, such as biking, hiking, and swimming.

- Stay up late, watching fireflies and looking for shooting stars.

→ Family, Friends, and Forests: Find out the nearest state or national forest and go visit it.

Do Your Part

Visit a local park or nature center. Ask children how people can care for the trees and other living things in this special place you are visiting.

Help build your child's vocabulary by using some of these new words in your conversations:

_____

_____

_____

_____

We are reading the following books. Check them out from your library, and invite your child to share them with you.

_____

_____

_____

SECTION 3

Meeting Neighborhood Trees

9 Parts to Play

OBJECTIVES

Provide opportunities and materials for children to:

- Compare human body parts with tree parts.
- Write about imaginary trees.
- Express feelings about tree parts and how they grow through music, movement, and art.
- Incorporate the knowledge they gain into their everyday world.
- Play outside in a natural setting.

ASSESSING THE EXPERIENCES

As you observe the children during the day, note the following:

- New vocabulary. In the children's conversations with you and one another, are they talking about tree parts?
- Questions. Are the children asking questions that show an understanding of trees and how their different parts help trees survive and grow?
- New ideas. Are the children able to see how people are similar to, yet very different from, trees?
- Integration of concepts. Are the children using trees and their parts in their art, play, and other creations, without prompting, in a way that demonstrates understanding?

WORD BANK

bark, branch, function, leaf, nutrients, root, seed, soil, trunk

STEM SKILLS

Communication, Creativity, Investigation, Nature-Based Design (making felt board tree), Organization (sorting tree parts), Problem Solving (designing newspaper tree)

OVERVIEW

Children make a tree costume and explore the parts of a tree.

BACKGROUND FOR ADULTS

A tree is a plant that lives longer than one growing season and has a well-defined woody stem that branches above the ground. Trees are usually big and tall when mature.

Trees have body parts just as people do: a trunk and branches, leaves, bark, roots, and seeds. Just like human body parts, each part of a tree plays an important role in that tree's life and growth.

Trunk and Branches: A tree's trunk is similar to the trunk of a human body, in that it provides physical support and contains vital structures for life, while the tree's branches or limbs are similar to our limbs. The tree's trunk, branches, and twigs support the leaves as they do the important work of making food. These woody structures contain small tubes that transport water and nutrients to the leaves (xylem) and that carry sugar from the leaves to the rest of the tree (phloem).

Leaves: These are the food factories of a tree. Using energy from the sun, which they capture with a pigment (chlorophyll), the leaves convert carbon dioxide and water into oxygen and food (sugars) through the process of photosynthesis.

did you know?

Forest Fact

Like humans, trees need all the parts of their body to work together to stay healthy. Each part—the trunk, the leaves, and the roots—plays a role in helping the tree grow. If one part gets damaged, the whole tree could die.

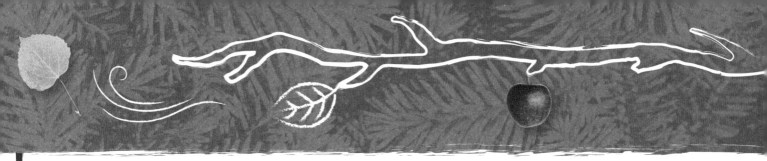

INTRODUCING THE THEME

Compare the children's arms, skin, and feet to a tree's limbs, bark, and roots. Have children stand next to a tree or use a picture of one.

Invite children to compare their body parts with the tree's parts. Ask: "How many arms do you have? What can you do with your arms? How many 'arms' does a tree have? What do you think a tree's arms do? What do you think your skin does? A tree has skin too. We call it bark. What do your feet do? A tree has feet too, though a tree can't walk around like you. They are called roots." Tell the children how to be a tree: "Stand straight and tall. Plant your roots, and don't move them. Stretch your branches into the sky. What would you do if a gentle breeze blew? What would you do if a strong wind blew? What would you do on a hot summer day? What would you do on a cold day?"

Bark: The bark is like the tree's skin. It protects the tree from injuries caused by insects and other animals, other plants, diseases, and fire. Depending on the type of tree, bark may be thin, thick, spongy, rough, smooth, or covered with spines. Just under the bark is a growing layer (cambium) that makes the branches, roots, trunk, and twigs of the tree thicker each year.

Roots: The roots help anchor the tree and absorb water and nutrients from the soil. All trees have lateral roots that spread out from the tree, and some trees also have a taproot that grows straight into the ground. As a tree's taproot and lateral roots grow away from the tree, they branch into finer and finer roots called rootlets. The rootlets themselves are covered by even finer root hairs. These root hairs absorb approximately 95 percent of the water and nutrients needed by the tree.

Seeds: These are plant embryos with protective coverings. They contain all the materials necessary for plants to begin life, including a small initial food supply. Seeds come in many different forms and shapes. Every type of tree has a special type of seed designed for the tree's habitat and method of distribution. Some trees produce seeds called nuts.

Like people, each tree is unique and beautiful in its own way.

Materials: *Are Trees Alive?* by Debbie S. Miller, one precut paper grocery bag (see diagram below) for each child, paper for making leaf rubbings, crayons, scissors, hole punch, yarn or string

Ahead of time, use the pattern below to precut a paper bag tree vest for each child. Children with limited mobility might be more comfortable getting in and out of a bag cut like a sandwich board that simply fits over their heads. (As an alternative, use lunch-size paper bags to make tree puppets instead of vests.)

Read *Are Trees Alive?* by Debbie S. Miller. After the story, talk about how trees and people are alike. Draw a large picture of a tree on chart paper, or use a felt board. With help from the children, label the tree with these parts: trunk, branches, leaves, bark, roots, flowers, and seeds.

Show the children a tree vest, and explain how they will use the vest to make a costume.

The children can make four or five colorful leaf rubbings by placing leaves (vein side up) under white paper and then rubbing over the leaves with the sides of paperless crayons. Children should cut out their leaf rubbings and punch holes in them using a hole punch. With your help, they should thread pieces of string through all the leaves and tie the yarn so it fits around their heads, thus making crowns of leaves.

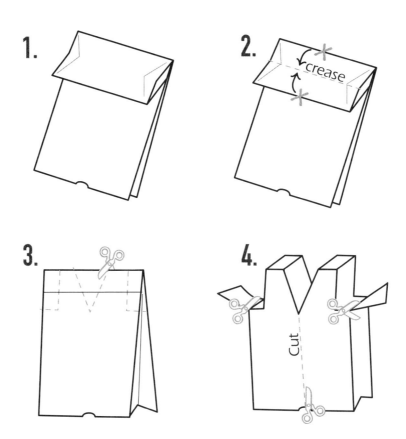

PROJECT LEARNING TREE®

Go outside together to make bark rubbings on the tree vests. Children can work in pairs or with an adult. While one person holds the vest against the tree trunk, the child can rub over the paper with a crayon.

When everyone is finished, call the children together to complete the costumes by following these steps:

1. Put on tree vests. Tell children that their bodies represent tree trunks. The trunk supports the tree. The vest is like the bark that covers the tree's trunk. Ask, "How do you think the bark protects the tree from rain? Insects? Diseases? Fire?"

2. Place crowns of leaves on children's heads. Discuss with the children how the leaves in the tree's crown soak up sunshine and make food (sugar) for the tree. Ask: "Do you think it would nice to be a tree and to be able to make your own food? If you were a tree, would you miss eating a lot of different foods?"

3. Give each child 4-inch lengths of yarn or string to represent roots. Ask the children to tuck the roots into their socks or shoes so their roots dangle over their shoes. Discuss how roots absorb water and nutrients from the soil.

4. Have the children hold their arms up over their heads to represent branches. They can stand close together and pretend to be a forest of trees.

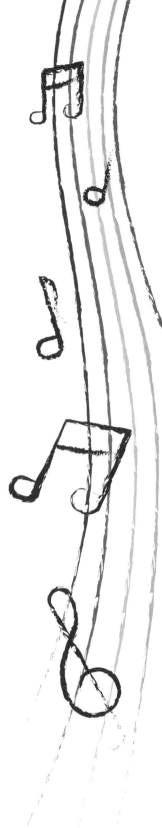

Music and Movement

SING A TREE SONG

Sing the following song to the tune of The Wheels on the Bus, varying the lyrics according to the season. Invite the children to suggest and demonstrate the movements for each verse.

The Roots on the Trees
Tune: The Wheels on the Bus

The roots on the trees go
slurp, slurp, slurp
slurp, slurp, slurp
slurp, slurp, slurp.
The roots on the trees go
slurp, slurp, slurp
all around the world.

The trunks of the trees grow
strong and straight
strong and straight
strong and straight.
The trunks of the trees grow
strong and straight
all around the world.

The bark on the trees protects the trees ...
The branches on the trees reach for the sky ...
The leaves on the trees make food from the sun ...
The seeds on the trees go twirl and plunk ...
The wind blows the trees back and forth ...

⟨3⟩ SING AND DANCE WITH BILLY B

Play Track 11: Yippee, Hooray! by Billy B on PLT's *Trees & Me* Playlist (scan QR code at right). Invite children to learn the lyrics and dance to the music. See Appendix C: *Trees & Me* Playlist for song lyrics and for tips on using this and other music selections.

GROW FROM A SEED

In an outdoor setting, show the children a variety of tree seeds (e.g., acorns, buckeyes, winged maple seeds, other seeds that are common in your area). Explain that you will read a story about what happens when a tree seed sprouts. Encourage the children to move their bodies as you tell the story. Read the following story out loud to them:

Imagine what it is like to be a seed and to grow into a tree. You are tree seeds, ready to leave the tree. You are shaped like a wing so you can fly on the wind. As you drop from the tree, the wind catches you and carries you away.

Can you feel the wind twirling you around? It lifts you up into the sky, and then you float through the air. Slowly, you drop downward and land gently on the soil. Lie down on the soil, and curl up tightly into a ball. You lie there, resting.

One day, raindrops begin to fall. They ping gently as they hit the ground. The wind begins to whistle and blow. Can you feel the rain and the wind? The water washes a little soil on top of you. You lie in the soil, drinking in the water. Soak it up like a sponge. Ahhhh, that feels good. You start to swell, and get bigger and bigger.

You get so big that you split open! A small root peeks out of the crack and starts pushing down into the soil. Wiggle your toes as your root creeps downward, growing longer as it reaches deep into the soil.

The sun peeks out from behind the clouds. It gets bright and warm. Can you feel the sun warming you? You are beginning to sprout. Slowly raise your head as your shoot pushes upward, growing toward the sunlight. Get up on your knees as you grow taller. Stretch and stretch—reach for the light. You're growing fast—you need water! Pull with your toes as your roots suck up water. Does it tickle as it travels up your trunk?

You start to grow branches. Push with your arms as your branches grow out of your trunk. Raise your arms higher as your branches reach for the light. Wiggle your fingers as you grow leaves to make food. The food travels down through your branches into your trunk. Can you feel it going down, all the way to your roots?

Stand up now. You are growing taller and stronger. You grow more roots to drink up the soil's moisture. Reach your branches toward the sun. Breathe in the air with your leaves. Feel the wind pushing against your branches. It lifts your leaves, and they twirl in the breeze. Feel the breeze swaying your branches back and forth, back and forth. Ahhhhhh! You are all grown up into a big tree now.

Take It Outside!

Take children outside to look for and document (with drawings or photographs) as many different leaves, tree bark, tree leaves, or seeds as they can. You might staple their drawings together to make their own "field journal."

Reading and Writing

GROW A TREE

Materials: Variety of tree seeds, heavyweight paper, glue, colored pencils, crayons, markers, or regular pencils

Invite the children to find tree seeds outdoors or to choose one each from your group's collection. Show them how to draw a horizontal line on their papers representing the surface of the ground and how to "plant" the seeds under the ground by gluing them to the paper, under the line. They can also color the paper brown under the line to represent soil. Ask, "What kind of tree do you think will grow from your seed? What color will the trunk and branches be? What color will the leaves be? How will the branches look? What kind of roots will it have?"

After the children are finished with their drawings, ask them to write or dictate descriptions of their trees. Display the drawings on a bulletin board along with a collection of tree seeds.

See Appendix H: Bringing Nature Inside for more information about using natural objects in learning activities.

PROJECT LEARNING TREE®

Exploring the Neighborhood

As you explore the neighborhood:

- Look for and explore tree parts. Children may find a leaf, rub the bark, and so on.

- Look for exposed roots along streams and in parks.

- Imagine how far the roots reach out under the ground.

- Find a tree with a trunk that takes at least two children to reach around.

- Find a tree that is the same size as the children.

- Look for seeds around the trees. Are any sprouting? Have any been chewed on by animals? Look for trees with unusually shaped trunks, branches, and twigs.

- Compare the trunks and branches of evergreen trees and deciduous trees.

- Find a small tree and try to count its branches and leaves. Try to imagine how many leaves are on a big tree!

 SAFETY! For safety information and other ideas for conducting learning outdoors, see Appendix G: Tips for Outdoor Learning.

Enjoying Snacks Together

BUILD A TREE

Recipe: 1 large pretzel stick, celery stick, or carrot (for the trunk); 4 small pretzel sticks, celery sticks, or julienne strips of carrot (for the branches); small pieces of broccoli, cucumbers, green pasta, lettuce, peppers, shredded carrots, or spinach (for the leaves); string cheese or cooked spaghetti (for the roots); raisins or sunflower seeds (for the seeds) soy or sunflower butter to stick the pieces together (optional)

Make a buffet table of tree parts. Put each part on a separate plate. Label the plates with the name of the tree part and a number indicating how many of each part each child should take.

Invite the children to put the right number of tree parts on their plates, to build a tree, and to eat it. As they eat, discuss the different parts of the tree. Ask, "How does the _____ help the tree? What is your favorite tree part? Why? Do you think these foods will help you grow big and tall? What does a tree need to grow big and tall?"

SAFETY! Be aware of any food allergies, dietary needs, or choking hazards for the children in your group.

Art

BUILD A "HANDY" TREE MURAL

Materials: Large sheets of paper, finger paints in seasonal colors (such as brown, green, and red), paintbrushes, scissors

Have each child place one arm, palm side up, on the table. With a paintbrush, have the child paint the inside of his or her forearm, hand, and fingers brown. Help the children press their hands and arms onto paper. Invite them to add leaves, flowers, fruits, and seeds to their trees by dipping their fingertips into different colors of paint. They can add roots by painting their fingers brown and making prints underneath the bottoms of their trees. Invite adults (e.g., principal, janitor, parents) to make trees too!

When the painting is dry, cut out the tree and hang it with the others on a wall to create a forest mural. Point out to the children how the "trees" are different shapes and sizes, just like people.

Discovery Table

⚙ SORT TREE PARTS

Collect a variety of items from trees (e.g., fruits, leaves, seeds, twigs). Label boxes with words and pictures of each tree part. Encourage the children to sort the items into the boxes. Ask, "If you were a tree, what kind of seeds would you have? What is your favorite part of the tree?"

⚙ DESIGN A NEWSPAPER TREE

As an engineering challenge for older children, provide pieces of newspaper, scissors, and tape and invite children to use the materials to build a tree that stands at least three feet tall. Provide a yardstick as a gauge. If they are stumped about how to begin, you might show they how to roll and tape pieces of newspaper to create their structure.

Math and Manipulatives

⚙ BUILD A FELT BOARD TREE

Make felt board tree pieces for children to put together. Provide a variety of sizes and shapes for branches, fruits, leaves, roots, seeds, and trunks to build interesting trees. Make felt board labels for each part. After the children have experimented with the tree parts, invite them to write a recipe for a tree. Using the tree part labels, children can decide how many of each part they need to make a tree (e.g., 1 trunk, 5 branches, 7 roots).

Explore Careers

Invite children to explore a green job that involves tree parts—FORESTER. A forester is a professional who takes care of forests or urban forests. Encourage children to pretend to be foresters and look for trees in trouble in the play yard or neighborhood. They can look for scarred trunks, bugs, or rotting bark. If they find a problem, they can check the nearby trees to see if they are also in trouble. (If you find any trees with big problems, like rotting and dead limbs that could fall, check with your local urban forester or an arborist about what to do.)

FORESTER

EARLY LEARNING STANDARDS

SCIENCE

Practices
- Asking questions and defining problems
- Developing and using models
- Planning and carrying out investigations
- Analyzing and interpreting data

Concepts
- Stability and change
- Structure and function

ENGLISH LANGUAGE ARTS

Practices
- Speaking and listening: comprehension and collaboration

Concepts
- Speaking and listening: presentation of knowledge and ideas
- Writing: text types and purpose

MATH

Practices
- Reason abstractly and quantitatively

Concepts
- Counting and cardinality
- Measurement and data

READING IS FUN!

Bulla, Clyde Robert. *A Tree Is a Plant.* **New York: HarperCollins, 2016.** This Let's-Read-and-Find-Out book follows the growth of an apple tree from seed to maturity. It explains tree parts and functions in simple terms. Ages 4–7. ISBN: 0062382101.

 Carle, Eric. *The Tiny Seed.* **New York: Little Simon, 2005.** In this classic story, follow a tiny seed on an adventure as it becomes a giant flower. Ages 2–5. ISBN: 068987149X.

Gibbons, Gail. *Tell Me, Tree: All About Trees for Kids.* **Boston: Little, Brown Books for Young Readers, 2002.** This large-format guide discusses the parts of a tree and their functions, the growth of trees, and the different types of trees. Ages 4–8. ISBN: 0316309036.

Holub, Joan. *Seed School: Growing Up Amazing.* **Seagrass Press, 2018.** While some of the seed friends in this story seem to sprout and grow up in just one season, one odd-looking seed with a cap takes many years to become the strong oak he was destined to be. Ages 4–7. ISBN: 1633223744.

Milbourne, Anna. *Peep Inside a Tree.* **London: Usborne, 2018.** This board book follows the growth of a tiny acorn into a beautiful old oak tree. Look under leaves and between branches to discover all kinds of creatures living there. Ages 1–3. ISBN: 147493384X

Miller, Debbie S. *Are Trees Alive?* **New York: Walker, 2002.** An introduction to trees that compares parts of a tree with parts of the human body. The story features people and trees from all over the world. Ages 4–8. ISBN: 0802788017.

Muldrow, Diane. *We Planted a Tree.* **New York: Dragonfly Books, 2016.** Simple text reveals the benefits of planting a single tree, both to those who see it grow and to the world as a whole. Ages 3–7. ISBN: 0553539035.

PROJECT LEARNING TREE®

Parts to Play

Things to Do Together

We are exploring trees, tree parts, and tree growth. Here are some activities you and your child can do together:

- Talk about how trees are like people and how they are different. Think about what we can learn from trees.

- Together, draw a family tree that represents your immediate family.

- Take a walk as a family to a place with trees. Let your child tell you what all the different parts of a tree are and what they do.

- Find as many different kinds of bark, leaves, seeds, and twigs as you can.

- Explore a tree with your eyes closed.

→ **Family, Friends, and Forests:** Visit a nearby forest and look for different tree parts.

Invite children to think about what they can learn from trees and allow time for them to practice "listening" to trees and nature. Encourage them to tell a friend or family member about something they learned from trees or nature.

Help build your child's vocabulary by using some of these new words in your conversations:

_____

_____

_____

_____

We are reading the following books. Check them out from your library, and invite your child to share them with you.

_____

_____

_____

Home Tweet Home

OBJECTIVES

Provide opportunities and materials for children to:

- Observe signs of insects and other animals living on, or eating, sleeping, or hiding in trees.
- Observe plants such as mosses and lichens that live on trees.
- Adapt a storyline by adding new characters and sounds.
- Express feelings about trees as habitats through music, movement, and art.
- Incorporate the knowledge they gain into their everyday world.
- Play outside in a natural setting.

ASSESSING THE EXPERIENCES

As you observe the children during the day, note the following:

- New vocabulary. In the children's conversations with you and one another, are they talking about trees as habitat for other organisms like insects, birds, and plants?
- Questions. Are the children asking questions that show an increased awareness of how plants and animals depend on trees?
- New ideas. Are the children drawing new conclusions or asking new questions about trees as habitats that are based on their observations?
- Integration of concepts. Are the children using the idea of insects, birds, and other species depending on trees in their art, play, and other creations, without prompting, in a way that demonstrates understanding?

WORD BANK

algae, forest, habitat, lichen, moss, snag, survival

STEM SKILLS

Communication, Creativity, Investigation, Nature-Based Design (making masks), Problem Solving (squirreling around)

OVERVIEW

Children discover how plants and animals depend on trees.

BACKGROUND FOR ADULTS

From their leafy branches to their tangled roots, trees provide habitats for a diverse variety of plants and animals. A habitat is the place where a plant or animal finds all the things it needs to survive, including food, water, shelter from weather and predators, and space to live and raise offspring. Many physical factors can influence habitat, including soil, moisture, temperature range, and light.

Different organisms need habitats of different sizes. A habitat may be as large as a square mile for a white-tailed deer or as small as a single plant for an insect. A tree may serve as part of an organism's habitat, or it may be the organism's entire habitat. For example, an oak tree may be just part of the habitat for a squirrel or a crow, but to the lichens and mosses growing on the tree, it's their entire habitat and provides everything they need. Trees sometimes serve as a microhabitat, which is a small, localized habitat within a larger ecosystem. A decomposing log in a forest is an example of a microhabitat that sustains a variety of animals and plants.

Even snags (standing dead trees) provide habitats for a number of different species. Tree frogs and beetles live under a snag's bark. Woodpeckers and other birds feed on the insects that live in snags. Chickadees nest in cavities created by woodpeckers. Squirrels and deer mice store food in holes and crevices there.

Take a close look at trees to see the many plants and animals that depend on them!

did you know?

Forest Fact

Forests are home to 80 percent of all land-based plant and animal species!

PROJECT LEARNING TREE®

INTRODUCING THE THEME

Materials: Tree parts that show signs of use by animals and plants (e.g., leaves with chewed edges, a log with lichens, bark with insect tunnels)

Encourage the children to describe their own homes. If available, use a dollhouse to facilitate the discussion. Ask, "What rooms do you have in your house? What do you do in your house? Where do you eat, and where do you sleep? Do you have a yard to play in? A park nearby that you visit a lot?"

Explain that animals and plants have homes too. We call a plant or animal's home a habitat. Using a real tree or a picture of a tree, ask, "Have you ever seen an animal using a tree as its home or habitat? What animals have you seen eating, sleeping, or hiding in trees?"

Display natural objects that show signs of animals and plants depending on trees, such as fallen leaves, twigs, bark, fruits, or nuts with chewed holes, tunnels, scrapings, cocoons, webs, mosses, lichens, or fungi. Allow time for the children to investigate the objects. Ask, "What clues do you see that show how animals use trees? What clues do you see that show how plants live on trees?"

FEATURED EXPERIENCE: A Nature Excursion

Go outside to find examples of animals and plants that depend on trees or shrubs in your neighborhood. If there aren't many trees, look for ways that plants and animals use buildings, bridges, or telephone poles as homes. Look for the following:

- Animals (e.g., squirrels, birds, insects) living in tree holes or leafy nests, hiding from predators, eating tree fruits or tree parts, and perching or nesting in tree branches
- Vines climbing up tree trunks to seek and soak up sunlight
- Lichens growing on bark
- Mushrooms growing on dead or dying trees
- Snags or fallen trees providing homes for many animals and plants

Take time to investigate a few trees up close. Collect some of the fallen objects. Take digital pictures of things that are too large to collect or that are still attached to the tree. Have the children do the following:

- Look around the tree for fallen bark, fruits, leaves, nuts, seeds, or twigs that might show signs of animal or plant life. Ask, "Who do you think left these clues?"

- Look on the ground for animal droppings that show animals live in the tree or eat the tree's fruits or seeds. Look—don't touch!

- Look on the bark for scratch marks caused by sharp claws or antlers.

- Look up in the branches for broken twigs, nests, and holes.

- Look at the small trees and shrubs near the ground for nibbled-on twigs and bark.

After exploring for a while, find a place to sit. Ask, "Do you hear any animals? Do you think they can hear us? What do you think they will do if we are very quiet?" Encourage the children to sit as quietly as they can while they use their eyes and ears to watch and listen for animals. When you observe a plant or animal, ask, "What do you think a _____ needs from a tree? How does this plant's or animal's tree home compare with your home?"

 SAFETY! For safety information and other ideas for conducting learning outdoors, see Appendix G: Tips for Outdoor Learning.

PROJECT LEARNING TREE®

GROUP EXPERIENCES

Music and Movement

 ACT OUT A STORY

Materials: *Good-Night, Owl!* by Pat Hutchins; animal masks (see Art) or puppets

Read the book *Good-Night, Owl!* to the children. Talk about the animals in the story and encourage the children to describe their personal experiences with any of them. As you talk about each animal, ask the children to make the animal's "voice."

Allow the children to choose which animal in the story they would like to become. Reread the story with the children acting out their parts using animal masks they've made or puppets. Children love repetition. As the story is read over and over, incorporate their improvisations and suggestions for change.

 SING AND DANCE WITH BILLY B

Play Track 12: This Bark on Me by Billy B on PLT's *Trees & Me* Playlist (scan QR code at right). Invite children to learn the lyrics and dance to the music. See Appendix C: *Trees & Me* Playlist for song lyrics and for tips on using this and other music selections.

Reading and Writing

WRITE A GROUP BOOK

Materials: Animal masks (see Art), crayons, paper, and other book-making supplies

After reading and acting out *Good-Night, Owl!*, ask, "What other animals have you seen in trees?" Encourage the children to choose an animal (e.g., amphibian, bird, insect, mammal, reptile, spider). Invite them to add a page to the story by drawing a picture and by writing or dictating text that follows the pattern of the story. To simplify the story, they can have each animal interrupt the owl's sleep individually rather than cumulatively. Assemble the new pages into a group book, make masks for the new animals, and act out your new story.

Enjoying Snacks Together

MAKE EDIBLE BIRDS' NESTS

Recipe: 1 cup "grass" (shredded wheat, crumbled), ¼ cup "strings" (coconut), 1 tbsp brown sugar, ¼ cup melted butter, fruit "eggs" (grapes, melon balls, or other round fruits). Optional: ¼ cup "sticks" (pretzel sticks, broken in half)

Preheat oven to 350°. Prepare muffin tin by putting cupcake papers or pressing foil into the cups. In a bowl, mix together "grass," "strings," and brown sugar. Drizzle in melted butter and stir well. Firmly press mixture into prepared tins to make nest shapes. Bake for 10 minutes. When cool, add "eggs" and "sticks" (if using). Makes 6 nests.

 SAFETY! Be aware of any food allergies, dietary needs, or choking hazards for the children in your group.

PROJECT LEARNING TREE®

FREE EXPLORATION

Art

 MAKE MASKS TO MATCH *GOOD-NIGHT, OWL!* **STORY**

Materials: Paper plates; hole punch; yarn, string, or elastic for tying on masks; scissors; crayons and markers; construction paper or foam pieces; buttons, craft sticks, feathers, pompoms, or other decorations; glue and tape

Provide dessert-size paper plates with the bottom one-fourth removed. Punch holes in the plate for attaching yarn (see diagram). Supply craft materials and encourage the children to make masks that represent animals. The mask is designed to sit on a child's forehead, with the straight edge of the paper plate resting right above the eyebrows. As a group art activity, you may also wish to design a tree for the story.

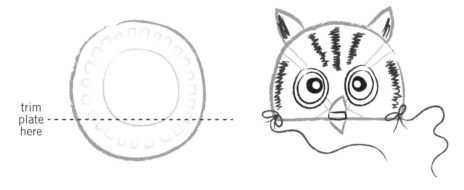

trim plate here

ADD ANIMALS TO YOUR TREE MURAL

In Activity 9: Parts to Play (see Art), children made trees by printing with their forearms and hands. Now they can add animals! Encourage the children to draw or cut out pictures of animals from magazines and to add the pictures to their handprint trees. Ask, "What kinds of animals and insects do you think live in trees? Where will your animal live (e.g., on the ground under the tree, in a hole in the trunk, on the leaves)?" Let the children add a variety of animals to the trees.

When they are finished, ask the children to step back and look at their creation. It's no longer a bunch of trees and some animals: this is a forest! Ask, "Have you ever visited a large area with many different kinds of trees and animals? What was it like to be in a forest?"

MAKE A LEAF BACKDROP

Using a large bed sheet, have the children make "leaf prints" by printing on the sheet with their hands dipped in paint. Use washable finger paints so the sheet will be reusable. Vary the color of the "leaves" depending on the season. Let it dry overnight. Use this leaf backdrop for Dramatic Play, picnics, and story times.

Take It Outside!

3 Look for and observe critters in dead leaves (leaf litter) or soil under a tree. Play an "I spy" game where you describe an animal you see and ask if children can see it. When you find something interesting, use a spoon to carefully lift the animal and place it in a jar or container to pass around for a closer look. After children look at the animals, be sure to put them back where they were found, covering them again with leaves.

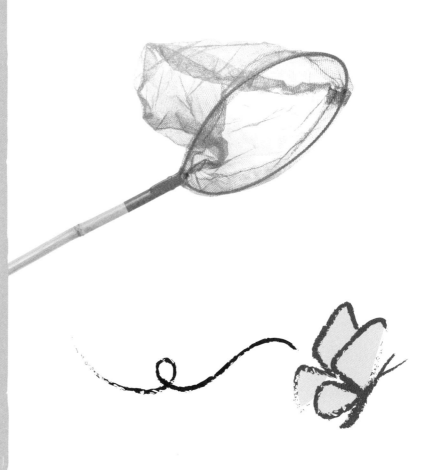

🌲 Outdoor Play

Try these fun outdoor activities related to animal habitats:

- Roll over a dead log together and look to see what's living underneath it.

- Put a white sheet under a tree and gently shake the branches over it. Have bug jars ready!

- Provide butterfly nets and large clear plastic jars with holes drilled in the lids. Catch and release!

- Look for nests in trees, being careful not to disturb nests or their contents.

Discovery Table

INVESTIGATE ANIMALS AND PLANTS THAT DEPEND ON TREES

Set out the natural objects from Introducing the Theme, along with magnifiers and field guides, for children to explore. Ask "How is a tree a home for a _____?"

 SQUIRRELING AROUND

Encourage children to pretend to be squirrels. Invite them to find and hide acorns and other seed pods. As an engineering challenge, encourage them to devise a way to move the seed pods from one place to another without using their hands.

Dramatic Play

3 **PLAY IN A TREE HOUSE**

Drape the hand-printed leaf backdrop (see Art) over a table or play equipment. Supply stuffed animals, puppets, and nest-building material. For older children, you might add plastic insects, eggs, and food. Ask, "If you were an animal and the weather became cold and rainy, where would you go? What would it feel like to sleep in a squirrel's nest? Can you show me? If you were a bird, what kind of food could you find in a tree?"

Explore Careers

Invite children to explore a green job that involves animal habitats—
BIOLOGIST. Biologists are scientists who study living things. Encourage
children to be biologists as they use "binoculars" (from Activity 1: The
Shape of Things) or magnifying glasses to look for animals living on a tree
or in the play yard.

BIOLOGIST

EARLY LEARNING STANDARDS

SCIENCE

Practices
- Asking questions and defining problems
- Planning and carrying out investigations

Concepts
- Biodiversity and humans
- Interdisciplinary relationships in ecosystems
- Organization for matter and energy flow in organisms
- Structure and function

ENGLISH LANGUAGE ARTS

Practices
- Speaking and listening: comprehension and collaboration

Concepts
- Reading: key ideas and details
- Writing: text types and purpose

READING IS FUN!

Bishop, Nic. *Forest Explorer: A Life-Size Field Guide.* New York: Scholastic, 2004. This book is a photo collage that explores and depicts many of the plants and animals that live in a forest. Ages 4–8. ISBN: 0439174805.

Brenner, Barbara. *One Small Place in a Tree.* New York: HarperCollins, 2004. A child watches one tiny scratch in a tree develop into a home for a variety of woodland animals over many years, even after the tree has fallen. Ages 4–8. ISBN: 068817180X.

Cole, Henry. *Nesting.* New York: Katherine Tegen Books, 2020. This stunning picture book follows two robins as they build a nest, keep the eggs warm, and protect their babies. Ages 4–8. ISBN: 0062885928.

③ Garnett, Jaye. *Who: Peek-a-Flap Board Book.* Rolling Meadows, IL: Cottage Door Press, 2016. Peek and explore in the forest, where you'll meet all sorts of animal friends. Ages 1–5. ISBN: 168052125X.

Hutchins, Pat. *Good-Night, Owl!* New York: Macmillan, 1990. This humorous story looks at an owl's daytime attempt to sleep in a tree shared with a variety of noisy wildlife. Ages 3–8. ISBN: 0689713711.

Sheehy, Shawn. *Welcome to the Neighborwood.* Somerville, MA: Candlewick, 2015. This stunning pop-up book takes readers from neighbor*hood* to neighbor*wood*. It introduces readers to several different woodland animals and explores their unique skills and behaviors that enable them to thrive where they live. Ages 4–8. ISBN: 0763665940.

PROJECT LEARNING TREE®

Home Tweet Home

Things to Do Together

We are exploring the plants and animals that live in and on trees. Trees are great homes (habitats) for birds, insects, lichens, mammals, and mushrooms. Here are some activities you and your child can do together:

- Visit a park or nature center and look for animals living, hiding, and eating in trees.

- Look at trees in your neighborhood for signs of wildlife (e.g., holes, nests, scat, nibble marks).

- Watch a tree for several minutes. How many different animals can you find? Look for amphibians, birds, insects, mammals, reptiles, and spiders.

- Make a flour "trap" to see if animals live near your home. On a smooth, flat board, deck, or off-the-beaten-path walkway, place a dusting of flour. Check for footprints the next morning.

→ Family, Friends, and Forests: Find out what animals live in our state's forests.

Do Your Part

Make a "bug hotel" to provide shelter for beneficial insects. To attract mason bees (which are gentle pollinators), fill a clean, empty soup can with paper straws cut ¼-inch shorter than the height of the can. Hang the can horizontally near a tree or bush. Search online for other ideas.

Help build your child's vocabulary by using some of these new words in your conversations:

_____

_____

_____

_____

We are reading the following books. Check them out from your library, and invite your child to share them with you.

_____

_____

_____

Community Explorers

OBJECTIVES

Provide opportunities and materials for children to:

- Explore places for living, working, and playing in their community.
- Experience how trees contribute to their community.
- Use words to describe their community and the trees in it.
- Express feelings about their community and the people who work in it through play and art.
- Incorporate the knowledge they gain into their everyday world.
- Play outside in their community.

ASSESSING THE EXPERIENCES

As you observe the children during the day, note the following:

- New vocabulary. In the children's conversations with you and one another, are they using more terms that describe neighborhoods and communities?
- Questions about community. Are the children asking questions that show an increased awareness of community and how it provides people what they need to live?
- New ideas. Are the children's experiences helping them form new ideas or refine old ideas? Are they drawing new conclusions or asking new questions about the people, places, and things that make up their community?
- Integration of concepts. Are the children using the idea of community in their art, play, and other creations, without prompting, in a way that demonstrates understanding?

WORD BANK

community, connecting, depend, helper, job, neighborhood, urban forest

STEM SKILLS

Communication, Creativity, Investigation, Organization (graphing kindness), Problem Solving (building community structures), Technology Use (using foil for foliage)

OVERVIEW

Children explore how their community—and the trees within it—provide things people need.

BACKGROUND FOR ADULTS

All forms of life—including people—need food, water, shelter, and space for living and raising offspring. Like habitats, human communities provide the things that people need to live, such as:

- Food—grocery stores, markets, gardens, and restaurants
- Water—community water systems (containing water from rivers and lakes) and wells
- Shelter—houses, apartments, townhouses, and other buildings
- Space—built structures and outdoor areas

A community includes all the people who live in a place, and it can be urban, suburban, or rural. Different members of a community exchange goods and services so that everyone gets what they need. We rely on many people in our communities who do different jobs, including bus drivers, construction workers, grocery workers, foresters, hospital workers, librarians, and teachers, just to name a few.

did you know?

Forest Fact

Urban forestry is the art and science of managing trees, forests, and natural systems in and around cities, suburbs, and towns for the health and well-being of all people.

INTRODUCING THE THEME

Ask children: "What things do you need to live? Where do you and your family get those things in our neighborhood (or community or town)?"

Communities also provide places to live, work, play, learn, shop, and meet. For example, office buildings and other establishments provide places to work; walking paths, parks, and gyms provide places to play; and schools and libraries provide places to learn.

Another important part of the community is green space, including the trees around our homes, on our streets, next to our schools, and in our parks. Known as the urban forest, these trees provide a range of important benefits for people and other living beings. The trees in our communities

- Release oxygen into the air.
- Create shade and control air temperature.
- Improve air quality by trapping air pollution.
- Reduce the intensity of wind.
- Store carbon in their wood.
- Improve water quality by filtering rainwater.
- Dampen sound, reducing noise pollution.
- Provide habitat for birds and other wildlife.
- Make our surroundings more peaceful and attractive.

Materials: Digital camera, printer, hula hoops

Lead children on an excursion around the block or through the neighborhood. Along the way, have them point out places where people live, work, and play. Using a digital camera, help children take pictures of the different places they see. Note houses, apartment buildings, stores, offices, libraries, recreation centers, playing fields, parks, and so forth.

Be sure to take pictures of trees, encouraging children to observe whether the trees are a part of the living, working, or playing places they found.

If the neighborhood isn't walkable or if you have children with limited mobility, you might ask the group to bring in photos of places in their own community. Or consider taking a virtual tour provided by an outdoor center, park, or community forest in your area. See Appendix B: Diverse Learners, Diverse Needs for more information about adapting learning experiences.

After you return, help children print out the photos and cut them apart, or display them electronically where everyone can see them. On the floor or ground, lay out three hula hoops or three jump ropes made into circles. Label the three circles:

- Living Places (with a picture of a house)

- Working Places (with a picture of a person working)

- Playing Places (with a picture of someone playing)

Depending on your neighborhood or group, you may want to include additional circles, such as Learning Places or Meeting Places.

One at a time, invite children to choose one of the photos and place it within one of the circles. (Be aware that not everyone will agree on placement, which is okay.) After all the pictures have been grouped, encourage children to think of other places in their community that could fit into each of the circles.

Share the pictures of trees and ask children which circle they would put the trees in. Allow different responses. Ask, "How are trees important for our community? How do trees help us? How do we help trees?"

GROUP EXPERIENCES

Music and Movement

SING AND DANCE TOGETHER

Play a song on the theme of community and friendship, such as The More We Get Together (Traditional), You've Got a Friend in Me by Randy Newman and Lyle Lovett, or We're Going to Be Friends by Jack White. Teach children the words to the chorus and invite them to sing and dance along.

CELEBRATE IN SONG

Music is used in almost every community on the planet to communicate and celebrate! Play samples of celebration songs from around the world, such as Jai Ho! by A. R. Rahman, La Bamba by Los Lobos, or Celebration by Kool & The Gang.

Encourage children to make up their own song to celebrate their group. Provide musical instruments from different cultures such as maracas (rattles made of gourds from Latin America), mbiras (thumb pianos from Africa), or castanets (clackers from Spain) and invite children to perform their song under a tree. Talk about people from the children's own community whose job involves music.

Reading and Writing

READ A STORY, WRITE A BOOK

Read Counting on Community by Innosanto Nagara or another picture book on community. Talk with children about what they would include in a book about their community. Give each child the sentence starter: "Our community (or town) has ...." and invite them to write or dictate their responses and draw pictures to illustrate them. Bind pages together to make a book.

EARTH MANNERS

Help each other

Be kind to trees

Respect all living things

Put trash in its proper place

EARTH MANNERS

Talk with children about how rules help people get along and keep us and our communities safe. Remind children about your group's rules and point out that the group is a part of the community. Encourage children to name rules to follow in their community, such as "Help each other," "Be kind to trees," "Respect all living things," and "Put trash in its proper place." Make a group chart of their ideas, combining or editing as necessary to include no more than five rules. Add a picture or icon to illustrate each rule. Invite children to act out each of the rules. After some practice, play a game in which you call out a rule and they act it out until you call another one.

 ## Exploring the Neighborhood

As you explore the neighborhood:

- **③** Look for trees in the community. Encourage children to use their senses of touch, smell, and sound to explore the trees. Invite children to share their ideas about what neighborhood trees give us.

- Look for people in the neighborhood doing different jobs. Encourage children to say how each of these people helps others in the community.

- Look for signs of wildlife that share the community space, such as squirrels, birds, ants, and other insects.

- Look for objects in the community that help people live. You might have children hunt for things in a particular category, such as Safety Things (fire hydrants, streetlights, or traffic lights), Fun Things (parks or basketball courts), Connecting Things (mailboxes, cell phone towers, or roads), or Beautiful Things (trees, flowers, or murals).

 SAFETY! For safety information and other ideas for conducting learning outdoors, see Appendix G: Tips for Outdoor Learning.

Enjoying Snacks Together

 FRIENDSHIP FRUIT SALAD

Recipe: Different fruits cut into chunks, yogurt (optional), large mixing bowl, big spoon for mixing, cups or bowls for serving, spoons for eating

Show children the different fruits and point out that they are like the members of a community. Each is good alone, but they are even better when they're mixed together! Invite children to help you make a friendship salad by stirring together the different fruits and adding yogurt, if desired. Or, have children create individual friendship salads by mixing their favorite fruit with at least one fruit that a friend likes. Or make a friendship trail mix using tree products like nuts, dried apples or cherries, and chocolate chips. Talk about how many of the things we eat come from trees and plants.

 SAFETY! Be aware of any food allergies or choking hazards for the children in your group.

FREE EXPLORATION

Art

 FOIL FOLIAGE

Invite children to paint a picture of a tree by dipping a crumpled-up piece of foil in green and yellow paint and then pressing it on paper to depict foliage. Encourage children to observe how different amounts of pressure on the foil creates different effects: light pressure makes airier foliage and firm pressure makes fuller foliage. When children are done painting the foliage, they may use a finger dipped in brown paint to add lines for the trunk and branches. Have them dictate why trees are important to them or to their community, recording their ideas next to or below the tree.

YOUR COMMUNITY, YOUR ART

Read aloud *Maybe Something Beautiful: How Art Transformed a Neighborhood* by Isabel Campoy and invite children to paint or draw a community masterpiece of their own. For further inspiration, you might borrow art prints from the local library or search online for great works of art that depict trees, bridges, buildings, and other community features.

Take It Outside!

Invite children to compare what it's like being in two different places: under the shade of a tree and in direct sunlight. Have them spend five minutes in each place. For each place, encourage children to describe how warm or cool the air is, how dark or bright colors look, or how they feel.

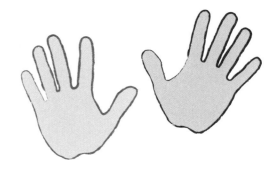

HELPING HANDS

Point out that people in communities depend on lots of different people to help them. Trace children's hands on various colors of paper and cut them out so that each child has two or more. Invite children to name some of the people that help their community. Have children draw a picture of themselves on one of their hand cut-outs and a picture of a community helper on each of the others. Assemble the hands into the shape of a large tree, with the community helpers forming the trunk of the tree and the children at the top of the tree. Point out that community helpers hold us up, and that children are an important part of the community, too.

🌲 Outdoor Play

Try these fun outdoor activities related to community:

- Invite children to create a "fairy" community using sticks, rocks, or other natural items they find on the ground, or with boxes, egg cartons, paper towel tubes, and other materials.
- Help children create a make-believe map of the play area, using their imaginations to name different places, like calling the sandbox "The Beach" or a corner with trees "The Forest."
- Bring out wooden blocks for building living places, working places, and playing places.
- Provide various colors of sidewalk chalk for children to draw a community mural on the pavement.
- **3** Play "Ring Around the Rosy" around a tree.

Discovery Table

⚙ BUILD COMMUNITY STRUCTURES

As an engineering challenge, invite children to use wooden blocks to create different community structures. Possibilities include (in order of increasing challenge): a house, a tower, a staircase, and a bridge.

PLAN A COMMUNITY

Make a base for a community model with pieces of colored construction paper for town blocks and use chalk to add roads. Then invite children to use building blocks or other materials to add buildings, trees, and other elements to the community.

TOOLS FOR THE JOB

Invite children to match pictures (or names) of community helpers to the tools they use. Examples include vet/stethoscope, farmer/shovel, forester/measuring tape, and librarian/book.

Math and Manipulatives

 ### GRAPHING KINDNESS

Encourage being kind to others while practicing math. Ask the children to bring in canned food or clothing to donate to a community organization, and have the children set a goal for the group. Help them create a graph to track their progress toward the goal.

COMMUNITY HELPER MATCHING GAME

Make a set of playing cards for a matching game on community helpers. Ask children for their ideas of different jobs in the community, including jobs that animals and plants do. Using images from the internet or your own drawings, create two cards for each community helper, such as two foresters, two teachers, two truck drivers, two trees, two butterflies, and two bees. Place all the cards face down and have children play "Memory" to match them up by turning over one card, then trying to turn over its match.

Dramatic Play

 ### PLANT PANTOMIME

Invite children to "plant" a garden using child-size rakes, a sandbox or plot of soil, and wooden or plastic fruits and vegetables. You might encourage children to identify which of the fruits and vegetables come from trees.

JOB ROLE PLAY

Provide children with a variety of props to role play different members of the community (e.g., mailman, police officer, firefighter, doctor). See Appendix D: Career Exploration and STEM Skills for information about exploring careers.

Explore Careers

Invite children to explore a green job involved in growing trees and urban forests—TREE PLANTER. Professional and volunteer tree planters are critical for maintaining forests and growing urban forests. They often work as part of a tree planting crew. Provide child-size shovels, trowels, watering cans, or other planting tools, and encourage children to act out being tree planters by "planting" and watering sticks.

TREE
PLANTER

EARLY LEARNING STANDARDS

SCIENCE

Practices
- Asking questions and defining problems
- Developing and using models
- Planning and carrying out investigation
- Analyzing and interpreting data
- Using mathematics and computational thinking

Concepts
- Natural resources

ENGLISH LANGUAGE ARTS

Practices
- Speaking and listening: comprehension and collaboration

Concepts
- Speaking and listening: presentation of knowledge and ideas
- Reading: key ideas and details
- Writing: text types and purpose

MATH

Practices
- Reason abstractly and quantitatively

Concepts
- Counting and cardinality
- Measurement and data

SOCIAL STUDIES

Practices
- Constructing compelling questions

Concepts
- Economics: exchange and markets
- Geography: geographic representations
- Geography: human–environment interaction

READING IS FUN!

Campoy, Isabel. *Maybe Something Beautiful: How Art Transformed a Neighborhood.* **Boston: Houghton Mifflin Harcourt, 2016.** Based on a true story, this book describes how Mira and a local muralist start a community project together, and how neighbors of all ages and races join in. Ages 4–7. ISBN: 0544357698.

Cumpiano, Ina. *Quinito's Neighborhood/El Vecindario de Quinito.* San Francisco: Children's Book Press, 2009. This bilingual book introduces children to the concept of community. It takes children on a tour through a young boy's vibrant community, introducing them to some of its members. Ages 4–7. ISBN: 0892392290.

Hopkins, H. Joseph. *The Tree Lady: The True Story of How One Tree-Loving Woman Changed a City Forever.* San Diego: Beach Lane Books, 2013. Motivated by the love she'd felt for trees since childhood, Katherine Olivia Session transformed San Diego's City Park from a dry hillside into a lush garden beneath a beautiful canopy of trees. Ages 4–8. ISBN: 1442414022.

Lamba, Marie, and Baldev Lamba. *Green Green: A Community Gardening Story.* New York: Farrar, Straus, and Giroux, 2017. In this sweet story written in rhyming couplets, the children of a diverse city neighborhood come together to build a garden for everyone to share. Ages 2–5. ISBN: 0374327971.

Malnor, Carol L. *Wild Ones: Observing City Critters.* Nevada City, CA: Dawn Publications, 2016. A curious dog named Scooter travels through an urban landscape, seeing—and not seeing—many wild animals. Charming illustrations draw upon real-life city scenes from across the United States. Ages 4–7. ISBN: 1584695536.

(3) Nagara, Innosanto. C*ounting on Community.* Salem, OR: Triangle Square, 2015. This counting board book describes different members of the community ("Three urban farmers, knee-deep in the mud") that help people live there. Ages 1–4. ISBN: 609806328.

Ritchie, Scot. *Look Where We Live! A First Book of Community Building.* Toronto: Kids Can Press, 2015. A group of friends work together to raise money for their local library. In the process, they learn about the places and people that make up their community. Ages 4–7. ISBN: 1771381027.

PROJECT LEARNING TREE®

Community Explorers

Things to Do Together

We are exploring all the ways that the people, places, and things in our community—including trees—help us live. Here are some activities you and your child can do together:

- Take a walk around your neighborhood to look for living places, working places, and playing places. Talk about how each of these places help people in the community.

- Locate trees in your neighborhood and look for signs of how people use them. For example, you may find tire or rope swings, treehouses, hammocks, or birdfeeders.

- Visit a grocery store, a corner market or bodega, a garden store, a clothing store, or another place of business. Talk with your child how it helps provide people in your community what they need to live.

- Over the course of the week, make a list of the people in the community who help your child. Invite your child to choose a community helper they might want to be when they grow up. Encourage them to play dress-up in that role or draw a picture of themselves in that role to share.

→ Family, Friends, and Forests: Talk about how city trees are like a forest.

Encourage children to express their gratitude to someone or something in the community. Help them write a thank-you note that describes how that person or thing helps them.

Help build your child's vocabulary by using some of these new words in your conversations:

_____

_____

_____

_____

We are reading the following books. Check them out from your library, and invite your child to share them with you.

_____

_____

_____

_____

Three Cheers for Trees

OBJECTIVES

Provide opportunities and materials for children to:

- Celebrate the gifts of trees.
- Collect and display tree products.
- Write about their favorite tree products or benefits.
- Express feelings about trees through music, movement, and art.
- Incorporate the knowledge they gain into their everyday world.
- Play outside in a natural setting.

ASSESSING THE EXPERIENCES

As you observe the children during the day, note the following:

- New vocabulary. In the children's conversations with you and one another, are they using more terms about tree products and wood?
- Questions about tree products. Do the children's questions show an increased awareness of the items and benefits we get from trees?
- New ideas. Are the children's experiences helping them form new ideas or refine old ideas? Are they trying to place the leaves on the tree (see Featured Experience) based on their experiences? Are they offering suggestions about new tree products?
- Integration of concepts. Are the children using the concept of products and benefits from trees in their art, play, and other creations, without prompting, in a way that demonstrates understanding?

WORD BANK

bark, benefit, celebrate, lumber, products, wood

STEM SKILLS

Communication, Creativity, Investigation, Nature-Based Design (decorating with tree products), Organization (sorting tree products), Problem Solving (experimenting with wood)

OVERVIEW

Children explore the many products and benefits that trees provide.

BACKGROUND FOR ADULTS

In addition to giving us wood, paper, food, and other products, trees are invaluable assets to both urban and rural communities. Trees beautify our environment and provide us with shade. They help to keep our air clean, prevent soil erosion, and reduce stormwater runoff. Trees also remove carbon dioxide from the air and store it as carbon, helping to reduce climate change.

Through the ages and in all corners of the globe, people have felt a deep connection to trees. Research shows that humans have a strong preference for wooded areas or landscapes with trees. In mythology, trees are sometimes depicted as the dwelling place of nature spirits. Trees are often planted to honor special events, such as the birth of a baby or the death of a loved one. Trees and forests have inspired countless works of art, architecture, and literature.

Indigenous nations across what is currently known as North America share the understanding that all living beings—including trees—are relatives, our family in the great web of life. For many Indigenous people, everything in the natural world is alive, from the soil to the wind. Having a good relationship with our relatives means respecting and appreciating the trees and other beings that make up our world.

did you know?

Forest Fact

Being outside among trees brings you many health benefits, and so does bringing trees inside! Exposure to wood indoors—whether in products, furniture, or design—offers many of the same benefits as being among trees outdoors.

PROJECT LEARNING TREE®

INTRODUCING THE THEME

Display a variety of things that we get from trees, focusing on food and wood products. (Older preschoolers might be ready to realize that paper products also come from trees.) Ask, "How are these things alike, and how are they different? Which things do you use every day?" Explain that all these things come from trees. Talk about the foods that grow on trees. Look at the wood grain in the wood products.

Ask, "What do you like about trees?" Prompt the children to think about benefits we get from trees. Here are some ideas to get you started:

- Wood products: houses, wood floors, lumber, baseball bats, toothpicks, wood blocks, wood furniture
- Food products: apples, cinnamon, chocolate, maple syrup, oranges, walnuts
- Paper products: books, newspaper, paper towels, toilet paper
- Other good things: clean air, places to climb, shade, homes for wildlife

People all over the world celebrate trees. In the United States, we celebrate Earth Day on April 22 and Arbor Day on the last Friday in April. Other celebrations around the globe include:

- Tree Planting Day (a public holiday), China, March 12
- Tu B'Shvat (the "New Year for the Trees"), 15th of the Hebrew month Shevat
- Tree-Loving Week, Korea, early April
- Midori Noni (Greenery Day), Japan, late April
- Dia del Arbol (Day of the Tree), Mexico, early July
- Maple Leaf Day, Canada, last Wednesday in September during National Forest Week
- National Forest Products Week, United States, begins the third Sunday in October
- Tree Dressing Day (which recognizes our responsibility for tree care), Great Britain, early December

From the everyday tree products we use, to the climate solutions they offer, to the global celebrations we share, trees are an important part of our lives!

FEATURED EXPERIENCE: Decorating Trees

Materials: A tree (e.g., a live tree outdoors, a tree branch with well-spaced branchlets and twigs "planted" in a 5-gallon bucket filled with sand, an artificial Christmas tree, a bulletin board tree), tree products (see Introducing the Theme), pictures of tree products, ornament hooks, copies of the Leaf Shapes template in Appendix J: Ready-to-Go Resources, markers

Cultures around the world decorate trees to celebrate how important they are. You can decorate a tree with small tree products (e.g., fruits, nuts, pencils), drawings of things we get from trees, or magazine cutouts of favorite things from trees. Use hot glue to attach ornament hooks to products that are difficult to hang.

⚙ Invite older children to sort the products. On a bulletin board, draw a large tree with three or four major branches. Label the branches Food, Wood, Paper, and Other Good Things. Glue or draw pictures of tree products onto the leaf shapes and cut them apart. For each, ask, "Which branch does ____ belong on?" If the children have different ideas about where to place the item, put it on the ground under the tree. Later, as the children learn more about the things we get from trees, they can agree on the branch where the item should be placed. If some products fit on more than one branch, make two "leaves" for those products.

PROJECT LEARNING TREE®

GROUP EXPERIENCES

Music and Movement

 SING AND DANCE WITH BILLY B

Play Track 13: These Trees by Billy B on PLT's *Trees & Me* Playlist (scan QR code at right). Invite children to learn the lyrics and create gestures to fit the music. See Appendix C: *Trees & Me* Playlist for song lyrics and for tips on using this and other music selections.

 PLANT A TREE WITH SONG

Collect tree seeds and sing the song Trees Need Water, Soil, and Sun, as the children plant and care for the seeds. Let the children help decide how to make the movements. Have the children practice together before singing the song.

> **Trees Need Water, Soil, and Sun**
> Tune: London Bridge Is Falling Down
>
> Trees need water, soil, and sun,
> Soil and sun, soil and sun.
> Trees need water, soil, and sun,
> To make them grow tall.
> Plant your seed deep in the soil,
> In the soil, in the soil.
> Plant your seed deep in the soil,
> And watch it grow tall.
> Give your seed lots of sun,
> Lots of sun, lots of sun.
> Give your seed lots of sun,
> And watch it grow tall.
> Give your seed lots of water,
> Lots of water, lots of water.
> Give your seed lots of water,
> And watch it grow tall.

 DANCE AROUND A TREE

Play Track 14: Tree Celebration Hoedown on PLT's *Trees & Me* Playlist (scan QR code at right), and dance an old-fashioned hoedown around your tree.

Take It Outside!

Invite children to spend time exploring two different places: a place without a tree (like the parking lot) and a place with a tree or trees (like a lawn, park, or wooded area). You might read a story in each place or do another activity together in each. Ask children which place they like best and why.

Trees Make Shade

Reading and Writing

CELEBRATE TREES BY WRITING A BOOK

Read *A Tree Is Nice* by Janice May Udry or another book about trees. Talk about all the things that trees do for us. Ask, "What do you like best about trees?" Remind the children of some of the products or benefits we get from trees. Look back at your group list.

Write a group book titled *We Love Trees Because...* or *Our Favorite Tree Things*. Encourage each child to choose a favorite tree product or tree benefit and to create an illustrated page for the book. Encourage the children to write or to dictate words that describe their feelings.

WRITE A THANK-YOU CARD TO NATURE

As children explore outside, invite them to name things they see, hear, taste, smell, and touch, and talk about what they appreciate about those things. Bring along paper and crayons for children to draw, write, or make cards to express their thanks and gratitude. See Appendix F: Traditional Knowledge and Gratitude Walk for more suggestions.

Exploring the Neighborhood

As you explore the neighborhood:

- Look for new trees and shrubs planted along sidewalks and boulevards. Observe how the trees are staked and protected.

- Watch for trees that have decorations, swings, or other "signs" that people love them.

- Count the number of trees that provide a shady place to rest and relax.

- Look for trees in trouble. You might find trees with scars on their trunks or broken branches. Look for tree roots that are pushing up under sidewalks or roots that people have hit with lawn mowers.

 SAFETY! For safety information and other ideas for conducting learning outdoors, see Appendix G: Tips for Outdoor Learning.

Enjoying Snacks Together

 ### DIP TREE FRUITS

Recipe: Toothpicks or forks, containers (to hold fruits, sauces, and toppings), tree fruits (apples, cherries, oranges, peaches, and pears cut into small pieces), sauces (chocolate sauce and tree nut butters), toppings (chopped nuts, cinnamon–sugar mixture, coconut, and powdered sugar–cocoa mixture)

Make a dipping snack from tree products. Provide a variety of tree fruits for the children to dip. Show the children how to use a fork or insert a toothpick into the fruit, dip it into a sauce, and then dip it into a topping. Talk about how each of the snack ingredients comes from trees.

 SAFETY! Be aware of any food allergies, dietary needs, or choking hazards for the children in your group.

FREE EXPLORATION

Art

MAKE A "WISH" TREE

Invite children to make a tree sculpture by scrunching and twisting a paper bag into the shape of a tree's base and trunk, and then tearing strips at the top of the bag and twisting them for branches. Provide different-colored strips of paper for children to write or draw their wishes for trees or things they appreciate about trees. Help them tie their wishes onto the tree to complete their sculpture.

PAINT INTERESTING TREE PICTURES

Provide each child a tree silhouette made of black construction paper glued to a blank piece of paper (see the Tree Shapes template in Appendix J: Ready-to-Go Resources). Encourage children to use chalk, paint, or other art materials to enhance it. Ask, "What is the weather like around your tree? How does your tree make you feel? How did you decide what colors to use for your tree?"

Outdoor Play

Try these fun outdoor activities related to tree benefits:

*   Plant a tree seed, seedling, or larger tree in your play area. Choose a native tree that will provide both beauty and food for wild animals. Check with a local forester, arborist, or nursery for ideas.

*   **③** Add seasonal decorations to outdoor trees.

*   Provide pots, soil, and tree seeds. See what happens!

*   Celebrate special "tree days!" (see Background for Adults.)

Discovery Table

DISPLAY TREE PRODUCTS

⚙ Provide common tree products that people use (e.g., apples, maple syrup, pencils, nuts, wooden utensils). Label three containers with pictures and words: Food, Wood, and Paper. Invite the children to sort the products into the containers. Your collection can grow as the children add tree products.

LABEL TREE PRODUCTS

Encourage the children to put a sticky note on each tree product they find around the room (e.g., books, bookshelves, chairs, rhythm instruments, toys, wooden frames).

Dramatic Play

TREE CHEFS

 Provide toy tree fruits (such as apples, oranges, and pears) and bowls, spoons, and pans for children to pretend that they are "cooking" foods made from trees.

CELEBRATE TREES

Invite the children to create their own tree celebrations or to act out why trees are important to them.

Woodworking

EXPERIMENT WITH DIFFERENT WOODS

From different places in your community (e.g., home improvement stores, construction sites, woodworking shops) ask for scraps or samples of various woods (e.g., balsa, cedar, maple, oak, pine, spruce, walnut). Provide magnifying lenses so the children can look closely at the wood. As an engineering challenge, invite children to consider: Which wood smells the best? Which is heaviest? Which wood is the hardest to dig their fingernails into? Which is the most flexible? Which wood do you think is the most beautiful? If you were going to build a _____, which kind of wood would you use? For more information, see Appendix I: Woodworking for Everyone.

Explore Careers

Invite children to explore a green job involved in keeping forests healthy—
FOREST FIREFIGHTER. Healthy forests give us wood and paper products,
as well as other benefits. Encourage children to act like forest firefighters.
Provide cardboard axes and child-sized shovels (used for clearing debris),
hard hats, and safety vests. Point out the importance of safety for
firefighters.

FOREST
FIREFIGHTER

EARLY LEARNING STANDARDS

SCIENCE

Practices
- Asking questions and defining problems
- Planning and carrying out investigations

Concepts
- Interdisciplinary relationships in ecosystems

ENGLISH LANGUAGE ARTS

Practices
- Speaking and listening: comprehension and collaboration

Concepts
- Speaking and listening: presentation of knowledge and ideas
- Writing: text types and purpose

MATH

Concepts
- Measurement and data

SOCIAL STUDIES

Economics
- Exchange and markets

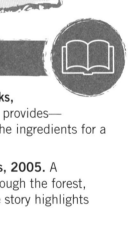

READING IS FUN!

Casey, Dawn. *Apple Cake: A Gratitude.* **London: Frances Lincoln Children's Books, 2019.** In this simple rhyming story, a child says thank you for the gifts nature provides—including apples from the tree and eggs from the hens—until the family has the ingredients for a delicious apple cake. Ages 3–5. ISBN: 071124779X.

Leavell, Chuck, and Nicholas Cravotta. *The Tree Farmer.* **Lorton, VA: VSP Books, 2005.** A grandfather who owns a tree farm takes his grandson on a magical journey through the forest, where trees become musical instruments, books, a baby's crib, and more. The story highlights the vital role that trees play in our lives. Ages 4–8. ISBN: 1893622169.

Marshal, Pam. *From Tree to Paper.* **Minneapolis: Lerner Publishing Group, 2013.** How does a tree become a book? Through photos and words, follow each step in the process from planting a tree to the final product. Ages 4–8. ISBN: 146770797X.

Mora, Pat. *Pablo's Tree.* **New York: Simon & Schuster, 1994.** Each year on his birthday, a young Mexican-American boy looks forward to seeing how his grandfather has decorated the tree he planted on the day the boy was adopted. Ages 4–8. ISBN: 0027674010.

③ *Thank You, Tree.* **North Adams, MA: Storey Publishing, 2021.** With every page of this board book, children see a wonderful tree, learn its name, and thank it for its gifts. Ages 1–3. ISBN: 1635864267.

Udry, Janice May. *A Tree Is Nice.* **New York: Harper & Row, 1956.** With a simple message, this book describes the importance of trees to people and wildlife. Ages 3–7. ISBN: 0064431479.

Underwood, Deborah. *Outside In.* **Boston: HMH Books for Young Readers, 2020.** This thought-provoking picture book explores the many ways that we are connected to nature and the outdoors, even as we live indoors. Ages 4–7. ISBN: 1328866823.

Three Cheers for Trees

Things to Do Together

We are exploring all the wonderful things that trees provide, such as food, wood products, fresh air, and shade. Here are some activities you and your child can do together:

- Go on a tree "treasure hunt" with your child. Search around the house for things that come from trees.

- Take a trip to a lumberyard or woodworking shop and look at wood from different kinds of trees.

- Visit a furniture store or music store and look for things made of wood.

- If you are a carpenter, whittler, or craftsperson who works with wood, consider sharing your craft with your child.

- Plant a tree seedling or seed to celebrate a special occasion or to recognize the importance of trees.

- Ask grandparents about wooden toys, tools, and utensils that they remember from their youth.

→ Family, Friends, and Forests: Talk about all the things we get from forests, including wood, foods, fresh air, and places to play.

Do Your Part

Some trees and plants have a rough life. Children can help care for them by watering during dry spells or spreading compost or mulch to provide nutrients. Ask at your local library or community center where you can help care for trees, plants, or gardens in your community.

Help build your child's vocabulary by using some of these new words in your conversations:

_____

_____

_____

_____

We are reading the following books. Check them out from your library, and invite your child to share them with you.

_____

_____

_____

APPENDICES

APPENDIX A:
Engaging Early Learners

The experiences in this guide are designed to excite young children's imagination, sense of wonder, and curiosity about trees and the natural world. If you are new to working with early childhood learners, consider the following guidelines when planning programs for children under six years old.

Young children learn best when you:

- **Facilitate active learning.** Young children learn by interacting, moving, playing, smelling, and taking things apart.

- **Focus on first-hand experiences, not on information.** Children need to handle objects, make their own observations, and draw their own conclusions. Abstract concepts, such as time, measurement, or cause-and-effect relationships are not appropriate.

- **Tell captivating stories.** You might start each experience with a read-aloud story. Each activity in this guide includes Reading Is Fun! recommendations.

- **Limit instructions to two or three steps.** Young children can remember only a few things at one time. Limit rules to two or three, as well.

- **Respond to physical needs.** Children will be more attentive if they are not tired, hungry, cold, or in need of a bathroom break.

- **Accommodate their egos.** Young children think everyone feels, thinks, and acts as they do. They are still learning how to share and be patient. Have enough tools and materials for each child.

- **Adapt as necessary.** Some of the children you work with will have physical or emotional limitations that require accommodation. For more information, see Appendix B: Diverse Learners, Diverse Needs.

- **Provide a safe environment.** Make sure there are no sharp edges or hazards in the learning environment, and don't let children handle breakable containers or small parts.

Young children benefit most from nature experiences when you:

- **Embrace play and unstructured discovery.** Young children learn primarily from play and exploration. The process is more important than the product.

- **Model research skills.** When children have a question that you can't answer, say, "I don't know. Can we answer that question by ourselves, or could we look in a book or online to find out?" When you ask them a question, wait for an answer.

- **Participate with them.** Model behavior and experiences. For example, be a scientist and record your observations, or be an artist and sketch what you see.

- **Rediscover your sense of wonder.** Share your favorite parts of nature with the children. Your enthusiasm will spread to them.

- **Go with the flow.** Early childhood classrooms can be unpredictable, and outdoor classrooms are even more so. If maple seeds are falling from the trees today, forget your plan and embrace the experience by choosing to play with seeds instead!

- **Model care and respect for nature.** Touch plants and animals gently. Carefully replace logs and stones after moving them. Leave things as you found them.

- **Think through safety and logistics.** Prepare ahead of time and know your objectives for the experience. Make sure outdoor sites are safe. For more information, see Appendix G: Tips for Outdoor Learning.

Children under age three (toddlers) benefit when you:

- **Choose age-appropriate experiences.** Look for this icon 🛑3 for experiences and recommended board books that are suitable for toddlers (children aged 1–3 years).

- **Take them outside.** Research shows that being outside stimulates toddlers' senses and helps build the synapses—connections between brain cells—that are crucial to cognitive development. A walk around a city block can be as stimulating as a walk in the woods.

- **Experience the world as new.** New and unpredictable sensations are enjoyable and exciting for children under age three. These experiences help them learn how the world works and enhance their language development.

- **Encourage sensory exploration.** Talk with toddlers about what they do, see, hear, and touch. Follow what grabs their attention.

- **Get dirty.** Making a mess is part of the learning process. Be sure that toddlers wear clothing that protects them from sun and cold. Bring extra clothing just in case.

- **Follow their lead.** Let toddlers lead the way by walking and stopping at anything that piques their interest. While they may not get very far, they will do lots of exploring. Bring strollers, wagons, or sleds in case children want to ride.

- **Redirect them as necessary.** Keep an eye out for anything that could be unsafe. Redirect toddlers to safe things they can pick up and carry.

- **Ensure their safety.** Check outdoor areas carefully and keep toddlers away from harmful plants and animals. Remove any choking hazards. Supervise closely to make sure toddlers do not put items in their mouths.

APPENDIX B:
Diverse Learners, Diverse Needs

PLT activities are designed to provide engaging and equitable learning experiences for a wide range of children. It is essential that early childhood educators know the children in their group and know how to accommodate for their unique abilities or challenges. Nonformal educators might have to quickly adapt an activity to meet the needs of children in their programs. Here are some ideas for making nature more accessible for diverse learners.

For all learners:

- Use simple and clear language.

- Show directions and desired actions using words, pictures, and concrete objects.

- Establish both verbal and nonverbal signals for calling the group together.

- Provide recording devices for children to log thoughts and observations.

- Put learners in pairs for explorations so they can help each other.

- Use praise and positive feedback.

For learners with cognitive or learning disabilities:

- Break down activities into small steps.

- Repeat instructions and information.

- Plan for extra time as needed.

- Allow learners to share discoveries through art, storytelling, and play.

For neurodiverse learners:

- Repeat directions several times and allow extra time for processing.

- Role model expectations.

- Encourage sensory exploration by providing objects with different shapes, colors, sizes, and textures.

- Allow for fidgeting. Provide play dough, squishy balls, or bean bags to help children relieve their sensory reactions.

- Allow children to opt out of specific activities if they prefer.

For learners with limited mobility or motor function:

- Choose accessible outdoor learning sites.

- Encourage them to use adaptive equipment, such as reachers for collecting items and free-standing magnifiers.

- Provide glue sticks (instead of liquid glue), adaptive scissors, and other accessible art supplies.

- If learners will be collecting natural items, give them bags with handles.

- Display collected items on a raised area for increased visibility.

For learners who are blind or have limited vision:

- Mark off outdoor areas with a guide rope.

- Use audio recordings when possible, such as bird calls or nature sounds.

- Provide a variety of magnifiers. Try a pocket microscope!

- Use a Braille labeler.

- Offer written materials in alternative formats, including Braille, large print, and audio.

For learners who are deaf or hard of hearing:

- Mark outside boundaries with physical clues, such as flags or chalk marks.

- Position yourself (and any sign language interpreters) so the children can see your face and lips when you are speaking (and the faces and lips of interpreters).

- If you go back and forth between bright and dark settings, allow time for students' eyes to adjust before you start speaking.

- Supplement listening activities with puppets, photos, or other visuals.

For dual language learners:

- Find out learners' experience in their home languages and in English.

- Label objects and visuals in each home language, with a different color for each language. An online translation app can help.

- Provide books on nature in the learners' home languages.

- Display photos, posters, product packages, and other visuals from learners' cultural backgrounds.

APPENDIX C:
Trees & Me Playlist

Nature is filled with music and movement, from the rustle of fall leaves to the musical calls of songbirds. For humans, music and movement are linked from birth. When young children experience music, they spontaneously begin to dance. The use of music, song, and dance activities builds the sensory–motor foundation for learning while engaging children's senses, emotions, and imagination about an object or experience.

The *Trees & Me* Playlist provides music selections that support the activities and experiences in this guide. It includes five songs from children's music artist Billy B. Brennan ("Billy B."), a professional songwriter and educator who focuses on environmental themes.

Unique QR codes will direct you to the 14 music tracks included on the *Trees & Me* Playlist. These QR codes can be easily read with most smartphone cameras. See plt.org/yc-playlist for the entire playlist. Sync your mobile device with a mini-speaker to optimize the experience.

May the *Trees & Me* playlist inspire you to share music selections of your own with young children!

Tips for Using the Playlist:

- **Listen to the music ahead of time.** Move to it yourself before presenting it to the children.
- **Practice singing the songs.** Do this before using them with children. Be dramatic and expressive in your singing.
- **Include simple instruments.** Use natural objects to create sounds.
- **Allow the children to be passive participants if they prefer.** Some children may need to observe for a while before they join the group activity.
- **Enhance listening skills.** Use blindfolds or invite the children to cover their eyes with their hands to hone their sense of hearing.
- **Repeat the songs frequently.** Each time you re-sing a song, make subtle changes. Repetition with minor changes engages children's brains.
- **Be an enthusiastic model.** Your attitude is contagious!

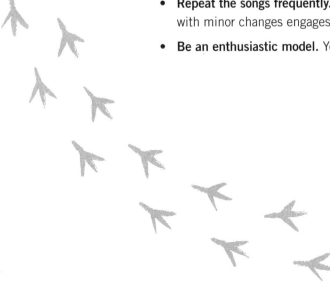

PROJECT LEARNING TREE®

PLAYLIST

See plt.org/yc-playlist for the entire playlist.

Track 1: Shape Walk (3:34 minutes)

Use with the "Dance with Leaves" experience in Activity 1: The Shape of Things.

"B-Roll" by Kevin MacLeod

"Tchaikovsky's Dance of the Sugar Plum Fairy" by Kevin MacLeod

"Kumasi Groove Flugelhorn" by Kevin MacLeod

"Sleep and Then" by Kevin MacLeod

"Bark Rap" by Steve Murphy (sound design)

"Flutey String" by Kevin MacLeod

(Kevin MacLeod selections used with permission from incompetech.com)

Track 2: Outside (1:25 minutes)

Use with the "Sing and Dance with Billy B" experience in Activity 1: The Shape of Things.

"Outside" by Billy B. Brennan

Well I get myself dressed, get my shoes on
Cause I'm gonna go where I belong
I'm gonna go to the door and open it wide
Let my family know I'm heading outside
Outside with all the living things
Outside to hear the birdies sing
Outside for discovery
Outside for my own curiosity

Jump down, look around
There's bees feeding on the flowers
New finds all the time
Stay outside for hours and hours

Well, I hit the trail
The sun does shine
The sky is blue and I'm feeling fine
My legs are moving
I've caught my stride
The air is clean and I'm outside

Outside with all the living things
Outside to hear the birdies sing
Outside for discovery
Outside for my own curiosity
Outside with all the living things
Outside to hear the birdies sing
Outside for discovery
Outside for my own curiosity

© Billy B. Brennan. Billy B.—vocals, guitar; Paul Seydewitz—bass; Hal Trapkin—percussion. See billybproductions.com for the many kids involved in the kid chorus.

Track 3: Neighborhood Sounds (1:30 minutes)

Use with the "Introducing the Theme" experience in Activity 2: Sounds Around.

Sound effects design by Steve Murphy.

Track 4: Nature Sounds (2:30 minutes)

Use with the "Introducing the Theme" experience and the "Featured Experience—Forest Concert" in Activity 2: Sounds Around.

Sound effects design by Steve Murphy.

Track 5: Getting in Touch with Trees (3:28 minutes)

Use with the "Be a Texture Detective" experience in Activity 3: Tree Textures.

"Desert City" by Kevin MacLeod

"Beach Bum" by Kevin MacLeod

"Divertissement" by Kevin MacLeod

"No Frills Salsa" by Kevin MacLeod

"That's a Wrap" by Kevin MacLeod

"Super Polka" by Kevin MacLeod

(Kevin MacLeod selections used with permission from incompetech.com)

Track 6: Flight of the Bumblebee (2:53 minutes)

Use with the "Smell the Flowers" experience in Activity 4: Follow Your Nose.

"The Flight of the Bumblebee" by Nikolai Rimsky-Korsakov (licensed from musicloops.com)

Track 7: Signs of Fall (3:01 minutes)

Use with the "Pretend to Be Dancing Leaves" experience in Activity 5: Fall for Trees.

"Untitled Rhythm" by Kevin MacLeod

"Divertimento K131" by Kevin MacLeod

"Beach Party" by Kevin MacLeod

"Modern Piano Beta—Jackhammer" by Kevin MacLeod

"Bumbly March" by Kevin MacLeod

(Kevin MacLeod selections used with permission from incompetech.com)

Track 8: Celtic Collection (2:33 minutes)

Use with the "Dance Around a Maypole" experience in Activity 7: Best Buds.

"Dance Ye Merry" by Adam Skorupa (licensed from shockwave-sound.com)

Track 9: The Four Seasons: Spring (3:20 minutes)

Use with the "Play Peek-a-boo with Spring" experience in Activity 7: Best Buds.

"Spring (Movement 1)" by Antonio Vivaldi (licensed from musicloops.com)

Track 10: Yummy, Yummy (1:54 minutes)

Use with the "Sing and Dance with Billy B" experience in Activity 8: My Tree and Me.

"Yummy, Yummy" by Billy B. Brennan

Now, yummy, yummy, yummy;
It's awfully sunny.
I can eat all that I want;
I can eat all that I want.
My leaves need the sun to make food for all of me.
They can only do it with sunshine energy!
Sunshine energy!

Now, yummy, yummy, yummy;
It's awfully sunny.
I can eat all that I want;
I can eat all that I want.
My leaves need the sun to make food for all of me.
They can only do it with sunshine energy!
Sunshine energy!

Now, the water comes up from the roots into the leaves.
They use what they need,
And the rest they sweat from their underneath.

With the sun and the water, the leaf makes food,
Then lets it go
Down through the limb, into the trunk
So the tree can grow!
Now, yummy, yummy, yummy;
It's awfully sunny.
I can eat all that I want;
I can eat all that I want.

My leaves need the sun to make food for all of me.
They can only do it with sunshine energy!
Sunshine energy!

Oh, yummy, yummy, yummy;
It's awfully sunny.

© Billy B. Brennan. Billy B.—vocals, guitar; John Seydewitz—percussion; Jeffery Hill—glockenspiel.

Track 11: Yippee, Hooray! (1:08 minutes)

Use with the "Sing and Dance with Billy B" experience in Activity 9: Parts to Play.

"Yippee, Hooray!" by Billy B. Brennan

Wet ground! Warm sun!
My life as a tree has just begun.
I'm so sure, I have no doubts,
Because my shell has cracked, and I have a sprout!
It's growing up, and growing out,
It's growing up, and growing out!
Yippee, hooray, I have a sprout!
Yippee, hooray, I am a sprout!
Yippee, hooray, I have a sprout!
Yippee, hooray, I am a sprout!

Wet ground! Warm sun!
My life as a tree has just begun.
I'm so sure, I have no doubts,
Because my shell has cracked, and I have a sprout!
It's growing up, and growing out,
It's growing up, and growing out!

Yippee, hooray, I have a sprout!
Yippee, hooray, I am a sprout!
Yippee, hooray, I have a sprout!
Yippee, hooray, I am a sprout!

© Billy B. Brennan. Billy B.—vocals, guitar; John Seydewitz—percussion; David Kenny—
12-string guitar; Susan Mackay, Pamela Albinson, Brendan Collins—kid chorus.

Track 12: This Bark on Me (2:30 minutes)

Use with the "Sing and Dance with Billy B" experience in Activity 10: Home Tweet Home.

"This Bark on Me" by Billy B. Brennan

This bark on me is my skin.
It keeps diseases out and tree juices in,
And protects me from bugs, dust, and wind.
Even though sometimes the bugs get in,
So the woodpeckers come,
And they make their mark,
Saying, "Knock, knock, knock!
We're hungry and there's
Bugs in your bark."
"Knock, knock, knock!
We're hungry and there's
Bugs in your bark."
But, if the bark breaks,
Disease may set in, killing me,
Just because of broken skin,
Just because of broken skin,
Just because.

This bark on me is my skin.
It keeps diseases out and tree juices in,
And protects me from bugs, dust, and wind.
Even though sometimes the bugs get in,
So the woodpeckers come,
And they make their mark,
Saying, "Knock, knock, knock!
We're hungry and there's
Bugs in your bark."
"Knock, knock, knock!
We're hungry and there's
Bugs in your bark."

Now leaves make food
That travels through the bark
Down to the roots
The food goes (phloem)
While minerals and water
Rise through sap wood
Up to the leaves
They flow (xylem)
And in between the bark
And the sap wood
Each spring
A new tree ring grows (cambium)
So if the bark is broken
In a ring around the tree
The food stops, the tree dies (oh no!)

This bark on me is my skin.
It keeps diseases out and tree juices in,
And protects me from bugs, dust, and wind.
Even though sometimes the bugs get in,
So the woodpeckers come,
And they make their mark,
Saying, "Knock, knock, knock!
We're hungry and there's
Bugs in your bark.
Knock, knock, knock!
We're hungry and there's
Bugs in your bark."

© Billy B. Brennan. Billy B.—vocals, guitar; Jeffery Hill—bass, vocals; John Seydewitz—percussion; Steve Murphy—keyboards, harmonies, percussion; Susan Mackay, Pamela Albinson, Brendan Collins—kid chorus.

Track 13: These Trees (3:23 minutes)

Use with the "Sing and Dance with Billy B" experience in Activity 12: Three Cheers for Trees.

"These Trees" by Billy B. Brennan

Every day people say, "What difference can I make,
What deeds can I do, what actions can I take?"
Well now is the time for you and me
To find a spot, dig a hole, and plant a young tree.

These trees releasing sweet oxygen,
These trees the monkeys and the birds are living in.
These trees limbs stretching up towards the sky
Whoa, these trees absorbing carbon dioxide.

Big trees, green leaves, deep roots in the ground,
The branches grow up, as the bark grows around.
And the flowers turn into fruit
Which falls to the ground.
The seeds sprout and take root.
Tree grows, sap flows, young tree grows big and old
Tree grows, sap flows, young tree grows big and old

Every day people say, "What difference can I make,
What deeds can I do, what action can I take?"
Well now is the time for you and me
To find a spot, dig a hole, and plant a young tree.

These trees releasing sweet oxygen,
These trees the monkeys and the birds are living in.
These trees oh their limbs stretching up towards the sky
These trees absorbing carbon dioxide.
So plant the tree that you prefer
The deciduous or the conifer.

Dig a hole deep, keep the roots straight,
Put that tree in the ground, water it and wait.
Water and wait, water and wait,
Water and wait, water and wait.
And as that tree grows, give it care
So it will thrive and grow when you're not there.
Yes, as that tree grows tall and strong
You can watch it grow all your life long.
Yes, as that tree grows tall and strong
You can watch it grow all your life long.

© Billy B. Brennan and Paul Seydewitz. Billy B.—vocals, guitar; Paul Seydewitz—guitar, bass
and percussion; Namu Luanga—vocals; Steve Murphy—percussion.

Track 14: Tree Celebration Hoedown (2:35 minutes)

Use with the "Dance Around a Tree" experience in Activity 12: Three Cheers for Trees.

From Wisconsin Project Learning Tree *Early Childhood Music & Movement CD*

APPENDIX D:
Career Exploration and STEM Skills

Introducing young children to a wide range of career opportunities broadens their notion of the work adults do, encourages imaginative role-play, and forms the foundation for career education. Each activity in this guide includes an Explore Careers suggestion, which introduces tree-related "green" careers through dramatic play or skill practice.

While the following 12 green careers are highlighted in the activities, there are many more careers related to trees and forests that you may want to explore with young children. If you also work with older audiences, visit plt.org/workingforforests for more career resources.

Highlighted Careers

- Arborist
- Biologist
- Chef
- Forest firefighter
- Forester
- Gardener
- Landscape designer
- Naturalist
- Nature artist
- Nature guide
- Tree farmer
- Tree planter

Developing STEM Skills

Career exploration in early childhood enables children to gain skills in science, technology, engineering, and mathematics (known collectively as STEM). These skills support youth development, no matter what career path the learner eventually chooses.

PLT promotes 10 STEM skills that are essential for everyone. At their core, these skills support hands-on learning that encourages children to ask questions, carry out environmental investigations, and develop new knowledge. They include elements of leadership, inquiry, and problem-solving, as well as skills related to human connection and care.

Skills with an asterisk (*) are used in numerous experiences within each activity in this guide. Others are identified in the sidebar and with this icon next to the appropriate experience: . Note that many activities include engineering challenges, which invite children to use problem-solving skills to design a solution.

Ten STEM Skills for Everyone

1. Collaboration

- Cooperating with team members
- Finding points of agreement or consensus
- Taking responsibility for individual contributions

2. Communication*

- Exchanging ideas with project partners
- Sharing project results
- Using different media to enhance communication

3. Creativity*

- Looking at a problem from different perspectives
- Exploring new ideas
- Learning from failures

4. Data Analysis

- Assessing the accuracy of data
- Presenting data in a useful format
- Identifying patterns in data

5. Investigation*

- Posing a question to investigate
- Planning and carrying out the investigation of a question
- Constructing an explanation based on findings

6. Leadership

- Leading projects or supporting a project team
- Developing a project plan and timeline
- Making decisions that are supported by data

MORE STEM RESOURCES

- **STEM Strategies:** Visit the PLT website for more opportunities to enrich STEM teaching and learning at plt.org/resources/stem-strategies

- **Self Assessment:** For older learners, try the 10 STEM Skills Self Assessment, accessible from plt.org/workingforforests

7. Nature-Based Design

- Finding inspiration in and from nature
- Recognizing that nature offers solutions to problems
- Incorporating ideas from nature into design

8. Organization

- Precisely following instructions, protocols, or blueprints
- Recording data accurately
- Keeping track of lots of different information

9. Problem Solving

- Defining a problem
- Using models to investigate a problem
- Designing solutions to a problem

10. Technology Use

- Identifying appropriate technology for a given application
- Using technology tools effectively
- Troubleshooting technology problems

PROJECT LEARNING TREE®

APPENDIX E:
Connecting to Standards

To help educators link instruction to academic requirements, each activity in this guide includes an Early Learning Standards graphic, which lists practices and concepts addressed in the activity for four subject areas: Science, English Language Arts, Math, and Social Studies. In addition, the following chart details K–2-level standards connections for all the activities.

In the United States, each state defines its own education mandates for schools, so exact curriculum connections vary by jurisdiction. However, many states use national standards as the foundation for their state-specific standards. The Early Learning Standards connections in this guide are based on the following national standards:

NEXT GENERATION SCIENCE STANDARDS (NGSS)

COMMON CORE STATE STANDARDS— ENGLISH LANGUAGE ARTS (CCSS.ELA)

COMMON CORE STATE STANDARDS—MATHEMATICS (CCSS.MATH)

C3 FRAMEWORK FOR SOCIAL STUDIES (C3)

Additional correlations to national standards for preschool education can be found at plt.org/academic-standards, including:

- National Association for the Education of Young Children (NAEYC)
- North American Association for Environmental Education (NAAEE) Early Childhood Environmental Education Guidelines for Excellence
- Head Start Child Outcomes Framework

Appendix E: Connecting to Standards (cont.)

K–2 EARLY LEARNING STANDARDS CONNECTIONS

SCIENCE	K-2 SPECIFICS	1	2	3	4	5	6	7	8	9	10	11	12
PRACTICES													
Asking Questions and Defining Problems	Ask questions based on observations to find more information about the natural and/or designed world(s).				■	★			■	■	■	★	■
Asking Questions and Defining Problems	Ask and/or identify questions that can be answered by an investigation.	★			■	★	■					★	
Developing and Using Models	Develop and/or use a model to represent amounts, relationships, relative scales (bigger, smaller), and/or patterns in the natural and designed world(s). [Models may include diagrams, drawings, physical replicas, dioramas, dramatizations, or storyboards.]		★		■	■	■			★		★	✔
Planning and Carrying Out Investigations	With guidance, plan and conduct an investigation in collaboration with peers.		★	★	★	■		■		★	■	■	■
Analyzing and Interpreting Data	Record information (observations, thoughts, and ideas).		■					■				★	
Analyzing and Interpreting Data	Use and share pictures, drawings, and/or writings of observations.		■							■	■	★	
Using Mathematics and Computational Thinking	Use counting and numbers to identify and describe patterns in the natural and designed world(s).	★				■			■			✔	
CONCEPTS													
Wave Properties	Sound can make matter vibrate, and vibrating matter can make sound. (PS4.A)		★										
Structure and Function	All organisms have external parts. Different animals use their body parts in different ways to see, hear, grasp objects, protect themselves, more from place to place and seek, find, and take in food, water, and air. Plants also have different parts (roots, stems, leaves, flowers, fruits) that help them survive and grow. (LS1.A)		■	■			■	■	★	★	★	■	
Organization for Matter and Energy Flow in Organisms	All animals need food in order to live and grow. They obtain their food from plants or from other animals. Plants need water and light to live and grow. (LS1.C)							★		■		■	■
Interdisciplinary Relationships in Ecosystems	Plants depend on water and light to grow. Plants depend on animals for pollination or to move their seeds around. (LS2.A)								■		★		■
Biodiversity and Humans	There are many different kinds of living things in any area, and they exist in different places on land and in water. (LS4.D)	■				■	■					★	
Natural Resources	Living things need water, air, and resources from the land, and they live in places that have the things they need. Humans use natural resources for everything they do. (ESS3.A)				★	★						★	★
Weather and Climate	Weather is the combination of sunlight, wind, snow or rain, and temperature in a particular region at a particular time. People measure these conditions to describe and record the weather and to notice patterns over time. (ESS2.D)						★	★	★	★			
Patterns	Patterns in the natural world can be observed, used to describe phenomena, and used as evidence.	★	★	★					■	★			
Scale, Proportion, and Quantity	Students use relative scales (e.g., bigger and smaller; hotter and colder; faster and slower) to describe objects.								■	■			
System and System Models	Objects and organisms can be describe in terms of their parts and systems in the natural and designed world have parts that work together.				★				■				
Structure and Function	The shape and stability of structures of natural and designed objects are related to their function(s).	★										■	
Stability and Change	Some things stay the same while other things change. Things may change slowly or rapidly.								■	★	■		

★ = Addressed in Featured Experience and other activity experiences
✔ = Addressed in Featured Experience only
■ = Addressed in other activity experiences only

K–2 EARLY LEARNING STANDARDS CONNECTIONS

ENGLISH LANGUAGE ARTS — K-2 SPECIFICS

	K-2 SPECIFICS	1	2	3	4	5	6	7	8	9	10	11	12
PRACTICES													
Speaking and Listening: Comprehension and Collaboration	Participate in collaborative discussions with diverse partners about Grades K-2-appropirate topics and texts with peers and adults in small and larger groups.	★	★	★	★	★	★	★	★	★	★	★	★
Speaking and Listening: Comprehension and Collaboration	Ask and answer questions in order to seek help, get information, or clarify something that is not understood.	★	★	★	★	★	★	★	★	★	★	★	★
CONCEPTS													
Speaking and Listening: Presentation of Knowledge and Ideas	Describe familiar people places, things, and events and, with prompting and support, provide additional detail.	★	★	★	★	★	★	★	★	★	★	★	★
Reading: Key Ideas and Details	Ask and answer questions about key details in a text.				■	■	■	★				■	
Writing: Text Types and Purpose	Use a combination of drawing, dictating, and writing to compose informative/explanatory texts in which they name what they are writing about and supply some information about the topic.	★		■	■	■		■	■	■	■	■	■

MATH — K-2 SPECIFICS

	K-2 SPECIFICS	1	2	3	4	5	6	7	8	9	10	11	12
PRACTICES													
Reason abstractly and quantitatively.	Reason abstractly and quantitatively.		★	★	■	■				■		★	
CONCEPTS													
Counting and Cardinality	Count to tell the number of things.					■				■		★	
Measurement and Data	Describe and compare measurable attributes.									■			
Measurement and Data	Represent and interpret data.				■	■						★	
Measurement and Data	Draw a picture graph and a bar graph (with single-unit scale) to represent a data set with up to four categories. Solve simple put-together, take-apart, and compare problems using information presented in a bar graph.				■	■						■	
Measurement and Data	Classify objects into given categories; count the numbers of objects in each category and sort the categories by count.					■	■	■	■	■		★	■
Geometry	Identify and describe shapes.	★											
Geometry	Reason with shapes and their attributes.	■											

SOCIAL STUDIES — K-2 SPECIFICS

	K-2 SPECIFICS	1	2	3	4	5	6	7	8	9	10	11	12
PRACTICES													
Constructing Compelling Questions	Construct compelling questions.											★	
CONCEPTS													
Economics: Exchange and Markets	Describe the skills and knowledge required to produce certain goods and services.											■	★
Geography: Geographic Representations	Construct maps, graphs, and other representations of familiar places.							★	■			★	
Geography: Human–Environment Interaction	Explain how weather, climate, and other environmental characteristics affect people's lives in a place or region.					■	■	■	■			■	

★ = Addressed in Featured Experience and other activity experiences
✔ = Addressed in Featured Experience only
■ = Addressed in other activity experiences only

APPENDIX F:
Traditional Knowledge and Gratitude Walk

Traditional Knowledge refers to the evolving knowledge of the local environment acquired by Indigenous Peoples over hundreds or thousands of years through their unbroken relationship with their territories. Handed down through generations, Traditional Knowledge encompasses the worldview of Indigenous Peoples, which includes ecology, spirituality, human and animal relationships, and more.

While Indigenous Nations across North America differ from one another in many ways, one commonality that they share is considering other beings besides humans to be our relatives in the great web of life. Having a good relationship with our relatives in the natural world means respecting and honoring all beings. By giving thanks to them, we can develop relationships of reciprocity, balance, and sharing, in which the needs of one being are not more important than those of another.

Use this Gratitude Walk to help children reflect on who and what is alive in the natural world, and to share their greetings to other beings through giving thanks.

Gratitude Walk

Find a park, forest, or other nature area where you can go for a walk with your group. Begin your walk by modeling a slow pace and quiet mind, taking time to notice all the life around you. Different cultures have different ways of thinking about what is and is not "alive." In many Indigenous understandings of the world, all of the natural world is alive.

Invite children to point out as many living beings as they can. Look for:

- Four-legged beings (squirrels, chipmunks, deer)
- Flyers (birds, insects)
- Swimmers (fish, some birds)
- Crawlers (bugs)
- All the different trees

- Flowers, mosses, and other plants
- Soil
- The weather (wind, sun, clouds, rain)
- Two-legged beings (people are part of the environment too!)

Talk about how all of these living beings are understood by Indigenous Peoples to be relatives, not just to each other but also to humans. They are our family! It is our responsibility to take care of them. Each of these beings has a role in the great web of life.

If you don't know what some of the beings are called, try to describe them based on what they look like, how they move, or how they make you feel. Encourage children to use their senses (seeing, hearing, touching, and smelling) to describe them.

As you notice each of these living beings, invite children to thank them out loud. Think about the role that each being has in the web of life. Do not disturb any of the beings around you; simply observe them, reflect on who they are, and thank them.

APPENDIX G:
Tips for Outdoor Learning

The outdoors—whether it's a play yard, a parking lot, a local park, or a natural area—provides a diverse and interesting "classroom" for learning. These places foster a sense of wonder, expand imagination, and deepen connections to the natural world. Both structured and unstructured time outside promote not only academic learning, but also mental, social, and physical health.

If you are new to outdoor learning, you may be worried about managing the group or about handling logistics. It helps to think of the outdoors as simply an extension of indoor teaching places. It doesn't have to be any more complicated than that! Of course, the farther afield you go, the more planning and forethought will be required.

What to Do

When you are planning outdoor activities, look for this icon ⬤, which identifies experiences in this guide that are particularly well suited to outdoor learning. In these explorations, children play, make observations, and conduct investigations outdoors.

Don't worry if the only outdoor space you have is a playground area or a city block. PLT activities are designed to be flexible. All activities suggest ways to get students outside and actively learning. The Take It Outside! boxes offer ideas for extending each activity's theme to the outdoors.

Tools for Exploring

Have handy some or all of the following tools to enhance children's outdoor explorations:

- Magnifying lenses, pocket microscopes, binoculars, bug boxes, or magnifying stands
- Notebooks, clipboards, or scratch paper for notes
- Child-size garden tools and gloves
- Flashlights
- Measuring tapes, thermometers, sundials, and windsocks
- Plastic food containers with holes in the lids for briefly holding small animals
- Field guides to local plants and animals
- Camera or video/audio recorder
- Pencils or crayons

Appendix G: Tips for Outdoor Learning (cont.)

Keeping It Safe

The benefits of outdoor learning greatly outweigh any presumed risks. Remember to:

Scout outdoor areas ahead of time.

- Check for any hazards like metal, broken glass, or litter.
- Be aware of traffic patterns and busy intersections.
- Know the locations of public restrooms, drinking fountains, and picnic areas.
- Learn how to identify and avoid potentially harmful local plants (such as poison ivy or poison oak) or small animals (such as centipedes or scorpions).

Be prepared.

- Know how to respond to allergies (e.g., bee stings, pollen) that your children might have.
- Bring an extra set of children's clothing, gloves, and a hat, just in case.
- Bring a backpack with a first-aid kit, emergency contact information for each child, water, snacks, and a fully charged mobile phone.

Dress for success.

- Make sure children are appropriately dressed for the weather.
- Protect everyone from ultraviolet (UV) rays with sunglasses, hats, and sunscreen. Check www.epa.gov/sunsafety for the UV index for your zip code.
- Model appropriate clothing yourself!

Teach safe behaviors.

- Remind children that classroom rules apply outdoors too! They still need to listen, take turns, and be kind.
- Teach children to "sit and stay put" if they become separated from the group. Role-play what to do if they get lost.
- Use a buddy system. When you call out "buddy check," have children find their buddies and hold up their hands. Conduct buddy checks and head counts every time you change locations or transition to a new activity.
- Make sure children know the boundaries of the learning space before they head off to explore. Mark boundaries visually when possible.
- Establish a signal—such as clapping, whistling, or using a birdcall—to call the children together.
- Teach children to be cautious when picking up litter. They should not handle any potentially hazardous items.

Exploring the Neighborhood

Neighborhood excursions are casual strolls that you and the children take regularly. Their purpose is to give children opportunities to observe and explore nature in their neighborhood.

Your first excursion could be a practice trip down the hallway or around the building. As you and the children become more comfortable, your excursions can grow longer and richer. For successful explorations:

- Rotate the line leader to give each child the opportunity to be the first to see things.

- Circle up the group to look at something interesting. This prevents crowding and allows everyone to participate.

- Emphasize both plants and animals. Plants are easy for young children to observe—they stay still!

- Allot plenty of time for the children to observe and talk about their discoveries.

Set Up an Outdoor Learning Space

For longer-term explorations outdoors, consider creating an outdoor learning space. A few simple modifications can transform a play area into a semi-permanent "outdoor classroom." To get started:

- Organize equipment and ensure that it is accessible to the children. Bins or a storage container can hold play equipment and tools for exploring.

- Provide child-size tables for workspace and snacks, and make sure there are benches or chairs for seating.

- Establish hand-washing and diaper-changing areas.

- Set up receptacles for dirty cups, trash, recycling, and compost.

- Store a basic first-aid kit outside.

- Use a wheelbarrow or cart for moving things between indoor and outdoor learning spaces.

- Set aside an indoor area to prepare children for going outdoors.

- Add nature-inspired art or decorations created outdoors.

APPENDIX H:
Bringing Nature Inside

Bringing nature into indoor spaces can greatly impact how we all feel, children and adults alike. Studies have shown that adding natural elements—even photos of nature—can reduce stress and heart rates, while increasing creativity and overall well-being. Bring the outdoors inside by incorporating natural objects and nature awareness into all aspects of your program.

Include nature in your activities:

- **Collect natural objects.** Children can display them on a "treasure shelf"; use them in art projects; and sort, count, and compare them for math activities. Collect pebbles, rocks, bark, seeds, twigs, leaves, acorns, pinecones, shells, fossils, and feathers. See the Take Care When Collecting section for more information.

- **Collect nature memories.** Encourage children to "collect" photos, sketches, sounds, and memories from nature.

- **Grow potted plants.** Try growing rosemary, mint, thyme, basil, or sage, which grow well indoors. Practice harvesting, cooking with, and eating these yummy herbs.

- **Adopt a pet.** Pets can help children learn how to care for animals and provide many opportunities for observing animal behavior and physiology. Good classroom pets include turtles, fish, and small rodents like mice and gerbils. Except for some insects, wild animals do not make good pets and it is often illegal to own them. Be sure to check your state's regulations.

Make nature part of your décor:

- **Make wall displays.** Showcase nature art projects in a designated display area. Hang a nature calendar and use it to track daily weather, moon phases, and other natural events.

- **Use the ceiling.** Hang cutouts of clouds, birds, bats, bugs, and other airborne objects above eye level. Construct mobiles made of twigs and leaves. Arrange glow-in-the-dark stars into constellations.

- **Make tracks on the floor.** Cut out animal tracks, place them in each animal's walking pattern, and tape them down. Deer, rabbit, and wolf are great examples.

- **Check the window.** Put a thermometer with a highly visible liquid tube and large numbers just outside a window. Set up a bird-feeding station outside a window, and keep binoculars and labeled pictures of common birds and animals nearby. Set a sundial in a sunny window, and teach children how to mark the shadows using a metal water bottle or other cylindrical object.

Use nature as inspiration:

- **Explore nature music.** Collect or build child-friendly instruments that replicate natural sounds (e.g., rainsticks, drums, birdcalls). Play recordings of nature sounds; try a different animal sound each day of the week (such as cardinal songs on Mondays, green frog calls on Tuesdays, and cricket chirps on Wednesdays).

- **Read about nature.** Stock bookshelves with nature-themed picture books, guides, and reference books.

- **Write about nature.** Provide nature journals for children to document experiences, ideas, and doodles.

Take care when collecting:

- **Know the rules.** Never collect rare or endangered species. Always have the landowner's permission before collecting material from an area. You may not collect any material from national or state parks, nature preserves, or land and water reserves.

- **Collect only what you need.** Leave the rest for nature and for others to enjoy. Try bringing just one clear plastic container for the whole group to limit the number of natural objects the group collects.

- **Do not disturb living plants.** Only collect flowers, leaves, seeds, or other plant materials from the ground.

- **Take care when handling living organisms.** Be gentle and stay safe; some animals bite or sting to protect themselves. If you keep organisms for any length of time, provide for their basic needs. Return all organisms to their original location as soon as you have finished observing them.

- **Leave no trace.** When the children finish exploring, show them how to restore logs and leaf litter to their original positions. Be sure to pack out all food and trash.

APPENDIX I:
Woodworking for Everyone

Building something useful with real tools is an excellent way for young children to develop their large and fine motor skills. The building process also supports problem-solving, creativity, self-esteem, and social skills. And working with wood allows children and adults to interact with an important forest product. Remember that all wood products come from trees!

Anyone can get started with woodworking using a designated area and a few simple tools. No formal training is required! See the Woodworking sections in the activities for specific suggestions for engaging your children in woodworking.

Tools

A woodworking area can start with a work surface and a few tools. Introduce tools one at a time. Over time, the woodworking area could feature the following equipment:

- Safety goggles
- Lightweight hammers
- Short screwdrivers with large stubby handles (straight slot and Phillips head)
- Pliers
- Hand drills (manual)
- Vises or C-clamps
- Large-headed nails, such as roofing nails
- Large screws
- Sandpaper and files in a variety of grades and sizes
- Wood glue
- Tape measures, rulers, and squares
- Carpenter pencils and notebooks for planning and sketching
- Small whisk broom and dustpan for cleanup

PROJECT LEARNING TREE®

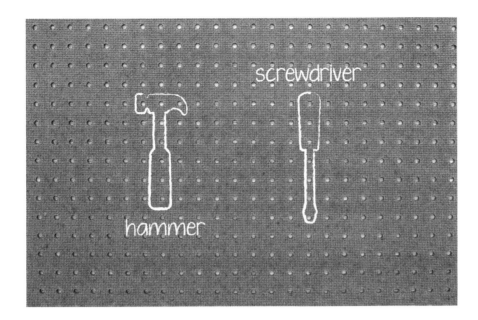

Tips

Use these suggestions for successful and safe woodworking experiences:

- Use a pegboard to hold tools. Trace around each tool on the pegboard and write the name of the tool next to the outline. This system makes it easier for children to return tools to their proper places.

- Introduce tools one at a time to small groups of children.

- Ask at home improvement stores, lumberyards, and construction sites for scraps of wood. Soft woods are best (e.g., pine, cedar, fir, redwood).

- Pound large-headed nails into stumps for practice. If your children are not ready to hammer real nails into wood, let them practice by hammering golf tees into Styrofoam packing pieces.

- To keep children from hurting their fingers when they are hammering, use needle-nose pliers to hold the nail. Children can also push the nail through a small square of paper and then hold the paper to keep the nail in place as they hammer.

- Use a vise or C-clamp (not hands) to hold wood for sawing, drilling, and hammering. Most injuries happen to the hand that is holding the material—not the hand holding the tool.

- When children are sawing, either both hands must be on the saw or the hand not holding the saw must be behind the child's back.

Safety Rules

Establish and reinforce rules for the woodworking area:

- Everyone must wear safety goggles, whether they are using tools or just watching.

- Tools have special jobs and can be used only for that job. For example, hammers are used only for hammering nails into wood.

- Tools and supplies must be put away after use.

- An adult must be present when tools are in use.

APPENDIX J:
Ready-to-Go Resources

The following copyright-free templates may be used to enhance children's *Trees & Me* explorations. They are specifically called out in the experiences identified below, but feel free to print and use them in other ways.

- **Tangram Puzzle**
  Activity 1, Math and Manipulatives, "Play with Tangrams."

- **Leaf Shapes**
  Activity 1, Music and Movement, "Dance with Leaves."
  Activity 12, Featured Experience, "Decorating Trees."

- **American Sign Language Cards**
  Activity 2, Reading and Writing, "Take a Listening Walk."

- **Tree Shapes**
  Activity 6, Music and Movement, "Make Tree Silhouettes."
  Activity 12, Art, "Paint Interesting Tree Pictures."

ONLINE SUPPORT MATERIALS
Visit plt.org/treesandme for additional resources to enhance the activities:

- **Family & Friends and Ready-to-Go Resources**
  Download printable Family & Friends pages and Ready-to-Go Resources.

- **Reading Is Fun!**
  Review comprehensive listings of all recommended Reading Is Fun! books.

- **Resources**
  Check out videos, webpages, simulations, and more online tools for teaching the activity topic.

- **Standards Correlations**
  Access correlations between Trees & Me activities and the Head Start Early Learning Outcomes Framework, the National Association for the Education of Young Children (NAEYC) Early Learning Program Accreditation Standards, and the North American Association for Environmental Education (NAAEE) Early Childhood Guidelines for Excellence.

PROJECT LEARNING TREE®

TANGRAM PUZZLE

The tangram puzzle originated in China over 1,000 years ago. It is made of seven geometric pieces: five triangles, one square, and one rhomboid (parallelogram). The seven pieces can be arranged to create different objects, including people, animals, flowers, boats, and more. Make your own tangram puzzle out of paper, cardboard, poster board, or wood, and then invite children to see what new shapes they can create.

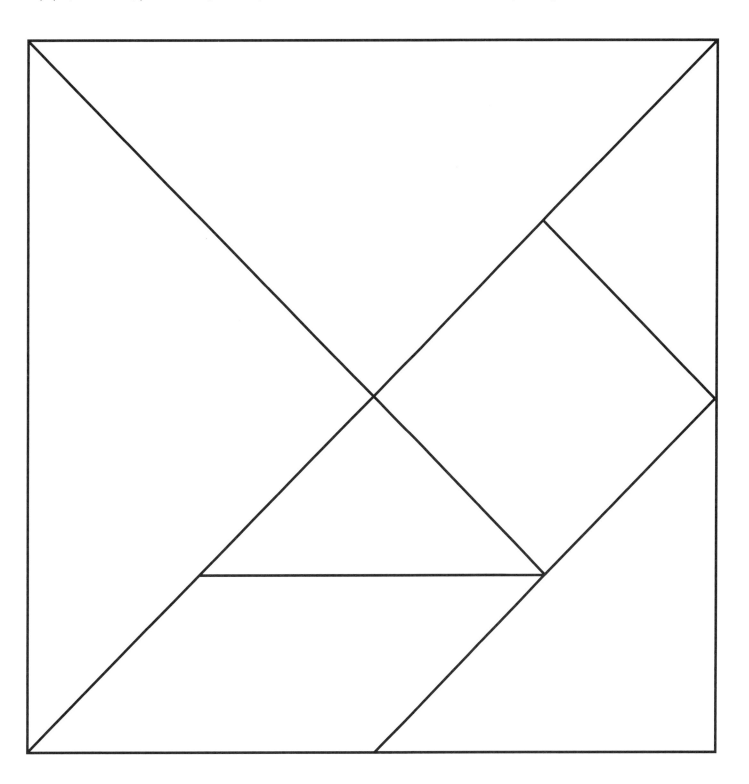

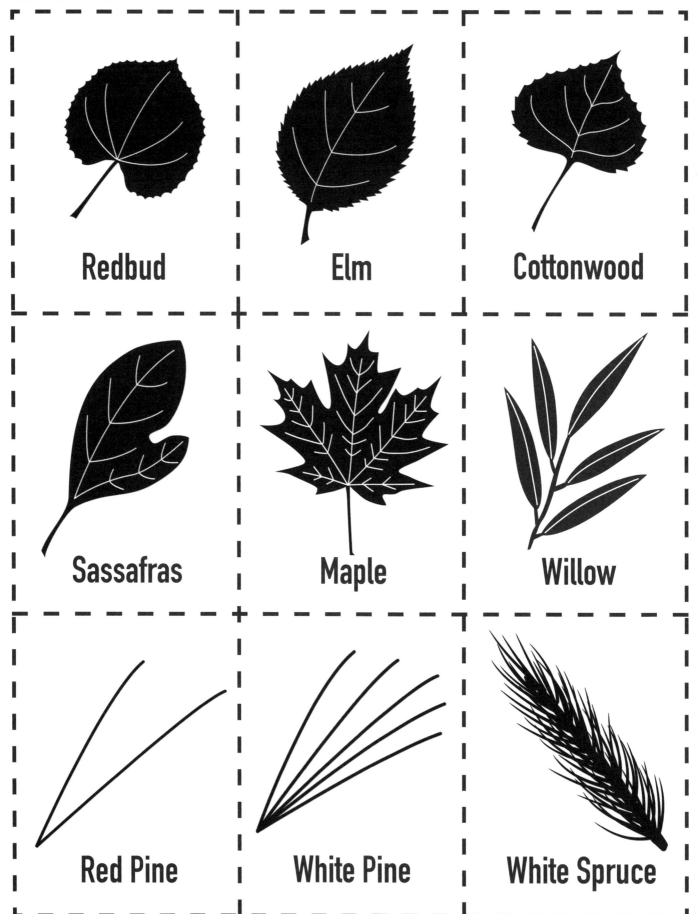

Redbud

Elm

Cottonwood

Sassafras

Maple

Willow

Red Pine

White Pine

White Spruce

AMERICAN SIGN LANGUAGE CARDS

These are a few signs related to trees and nature. If you are interested in more, visit signasl.org to access a free online American Sign Language dictionary.

tree

Make a tree with your right hand and shake it back and forth.

animal

Put your fingertips on your chest and rock your hands back and forth.

bug

Put your thumb on your nose and bend and straighten your first two fingers a few times.

bird

Open and close your thumb and index finger twice.

rain

Move your hands downward while opening and closing your fingers.

wind

Sway your hands back and forth - the stronger the wind, the faster the movement.

TREE SHAPES

Spruce

Pinyon Pine

Cedar

Maple

Oak

Elm

Willow

Beech

Palm

APPENDIX K:
Acknowledgments

Project Learning Tree gratefully acknowledges those who volunteered their time to review and pilot test this resource.

PROJECT DIRECTOR
Jaclyn Stallard
Director, Curriculum, SFI/PLT

CONTENT EXPERTS
Joanne Alex
Stillwater Montessori School (Retired), ME

Judy Bliss
PLT, WET, and WILD Facilitator (Retired), NY

Leanne Coyle
South Carolina Department of Social
Services, SC

Tarneshia Evans
Richmond City Parks & Recreation, VA

Ronda Hawkins
Sandhills Community College, NC

Linda Kinney
North Carolina Zoo, NC

Angel Mayberry
ESU 7 Early Learning Connection, NE

Kathy Osborne
North Carolina Zoo, NC

Tia Prostko
Program for Infant and Toddler Care, SC

Cara Small
ESU 6 Early Learning Connection, NE

PRACTITIONER REVIEWERS
Greta Combs
Tree Hill Nature Center, FL

Kathryn Fischer
Michigan State University, MI

Tina Fleming
Wakulla County Schools, FL

Ronda Hawkins
Sandhills Community College, NC

Jessica Kratz
Greenbelt Nature Center, NY

Tammi Remsburg
Cabarrus Soil and Water Conservation
District, NC

Mary Ronan
New York State Department of Environmental
Conservation, NY

WRITER & EDITOR
Leslie Comnes
Writing for Education, Portland, OR

Heather Sisan
Copyeditor, Rockville, MD

FOCUS GROUP PARTICIPANTS
Danielle Ardrey
Colorado State Forest Service, CO

Rob Beadel
Arkansas Forestry Association, AR

Beth Bernard
Connecticut Forest and Park Association, CT

Denise Buck
Pacific Education Institute, WA

Linda Carnell
West Virginia Division of Forestry, WV

Cynthia Chavez
University of California, CA

Aubrey Davis
North Dakota State University, ND

Jean Devlin
Pennsylvania Bureau of Forestry, PA

Laura Duffey
Minnesota Department of Natural Resources, MN

Nicole Filizetti
University of Wisconsin – Stevens Point, WI

Beth Foley
South Carolina Forestry Commission, SC

Cindy Frenzel
Virginia Department of Forestry, VA

Molly Gillespie
Alaska Association of Conservation Districts, AK

Jessie Halverson
Wyoming PLT, WY

Jack Hilgert
Nebraska Forest Service, NE

Ashley Hoffman
Kentucky Association for Environmental
Education, KY

Yasmeen Hossain
Oregon Natural Resources Education
Program, OR

Jessica Ireland
University of Florida, FL

Jonathan LaBonte
Maine TREE Foundation, ME

Carissa Longo
Pennsylvania Department of Conservation
& Natural Resources, NY

LeeAnn Mikkelson
Oregon Natural Resources Education
Program, OR

Katie Navin
Colorado Alliance for Environmental
Education, CO

Cecilia Ochoa Blackaller
Profauna, Mexico

Jennifer Okerlund
Idaho Forest Products Commission, ID

Kelli Parke-Buckner
Environmental Education Association of
Illinois, IL

Hanna Pinneo
Nebraska Forest Service, NE

Alex Porpora
Utah Society for Environmental Education, UT

Mo Rice
Oklahoma Forestry Services, OK

Donna Rogler
Indiana Department of Natural Resources, IN

Matt Schnabel
South Carolina Forestry Commission, SC

Emma Skinner
Mississippi Forestry Association, MS

Ashley Smith
Alabama Forestry Association, AL

Renee Strnad
North Carolina State University, NC

Ada Takacs
Michigan Department of Natural Resources, MI

Betsy Ukeritis
New York State Department of Environmental
Conservation, NY

Emmy Westlake
University of California, CA

Mary Westlund
Maryland Association for Environmental and
Outdoor Education, MD

Sue Wintering
Ohio Department of Natural Resources, OH

Chelsea York
Georgia Forestry Commission, GA

Michelle Youngquist
Idaho Forest Products Commission, ID

In addition, PLT State Coordinators, Education
Operating Committee members, and SFI
staff contributed to the development of this
guide. We're grateful to all the educators,
curriculum specialists, technical experts,
resource professionals, and partners who help
support, develop, and deliver high-quality
environmental education.

Notes:

Notes:

Strength in Our Network

Our PLT network, spanning all 50 states and international locations, provides educators with hands-on professional development, state-specific supplements that address local academic standards and environmental issues, and customized assistance for adopting environmental education. The link below provides contact information for the PLT coordinator in your state. Please consider this an invitation to reach out and get involved today!

Contact your PLT State Coordinator for:

- Local resources and assistance

- Ideas for incorporating environmental education and outdoor learning into your program

- Connections to mentor teachers, community members, and natural resource professionals

- Information about in-person professional development events near you

- Guidance to become a PLT professional development facilitator

Experience PLT's professional development to:

- Gain new teaching skills, deepen your content knowledge, and become comfortable teaching outdoors

- Receive instructional materials tailored to your state's standards

- Experience PLT activities, develop an action plan, and get lesson planning tips specific to your setting

- Get access to a network of professionals and support

- Earn continuing education credits

GET CONNECTED TODAY

https://www.plt.org/yourstate

PROJECT LEARNING TREE®